HAUS CURIOSITIES

The London Problem

About the Author

Jack Brown is Lecturer in London Studies at King's College London. From 2016–17, he was the first-ever Researcher in Residence at No. 10 Downing Street. Brown is the author of *No. 10: The Geography of Power at Downing Street* and *London's Mayor at 20: Governing a Global City in the 21st Century*.

Jack Brown

THE LONDON PROBLEM

What Britain Gets Wrong About Its Capital City

First published by Haus Publishing in 2021
4 Cinnamon Row
London SW11 3TW
www.hauspublishing.com

A CIP catalogue record for this book is
available from the British Library

Print ISBN: 978-1-913368-14-2
Ebook ISBN: 978-1-913368-15-9

Typeset in Garamond by MacGuru Ltd

Printed in Czech Republic

Contents

Preface

> Why, Sir, you find no man, at all intellectual, who is willing to leave London. No, Sir, when a man is tired of London, he is tired of life; for there is in London all that life can afford.
>
> Samuel Johnson, 1777[1]

> You guys should get out of London. Go and talk to people who are not rich remainers.
>
> Dominic Cummings, chief adviser to the prime minister, 2019[2]

The London 'problem'

It is now approaching 200 years since William Cobbett, radical pamphleteer and advocate for rural England, famously described London as 'the Great Wen', an ever-expanding and ugly cyst sucking the lifeblood of its nation. But recent years have seen national politicians return to this theme, describing London as the 'dark star of the economy' and a 'giant suction machine draining the life out of the rest of the country'.[3]

The more things change, it seems, the more they stay the same. The economic gap between capital and country grows ever larger, and London's powerful draw continues to cause concern. But today's anti-London sentiment has acquired additional new strands: political, economic, historical, and cultural. Some are based on legitimate grievances and concerns, others on prejudice and misconceptions. All have become interwoven – sometimes deliberately, sometimes accidentally – into a complex knot of resentment against the capital.

This book attempts to untangle some of these strands, however briefly, to try to better understand them. It begins with an overview of the facts, before undertaking a historical review of past attempts to address London's perceived dominance within the UK. Next, it explores public perceptions and the relationship between rhetoric and reality. In closing, it considers the impact of the coronavirus pandemic, which arrived between this book's conception and its delivery, and some possibilities for the future.

This book

This addition to Haus's Curiosities series draws heavily on my research for a report entitled *London, UK*, conducted in 2018 for Centre for London. I am extremely grateful to Centre for London for the opportunity to spend time getting to know this subject and for its support – particularly that of Richard Brown (no relation). The views expressed in this book, however, are very much the author's own.

In this book, I have identified several threads of anti-London sentiment that interweave, overlap, and are often incorrectly identified or mistaken for one another. This, to some extent, is the problem.

'London' means different things to different people. It has become a catch-all word for whatever it is that people don't like, from government to globalisation and much more besides. I have attempted to deal with several (if not all) of these interpretations of 'London', but I too make the mistake of flicking between different meanings and conceptualisations – political, economic, and cultural – of what is, ultimately, a place populated by people. These 9 million or so people are all very different to one another, as are their 57 million fellow Brits. Sometimes it is useful to observe certain traits and place these people into various groups, but as individuals they defy stereotypes as often as they fit them.

London itself is so large and multifaceted that it is tempting to cherry-pick facts and ignore others for the sake of building an argument 'for' or 'against' the city and its people. No doubt I am as guilty as others in doing this, but I have tried to be balanced and accept nuance. Ultimately, we must accept that this is one point of view. Others are available. (But mine – just to be clear – is the right one.)

Personal note

On that note, I must include a disclaimer. I am a life-long north-east Londoner. I am a 'somewhere' person, and I have lived in one London borough my entire life. I feel a strong attachment to my place. My football team, through my family, is Arsenal. People around the world support Arsenal, but I think that my connection to the club is real; theirs is just a hobby. They could have picked any team. I couldn't.

This is how I feel about London, or at least my patch of north-east London. But this is clearly not true (nor, for that matter, is it really true of football clubs). Friends and family have moved, generally outwards, whether to find more space, a change of lifestyle, or a better stand-ard of living. Others have moved in. I could move too. I don't own this place, and it is changing rapidly even in front of my eyes. Parts are almost unrecognisable to me, already, at the age of thirty-four. Yet still I cling on to this patch of land.

It has a lot going for it. And I have been very fortunate

to be able to stay here as the place has changed around me. At times, it can feel like I am running to stand still as prices and properties (and property prices) grow ever upwards and new shops pop up left, right, and centre, selling beard oil and bacon jam. It would help me, as a Londoner, if the capital's magnetic attraction to people, money, and opportunity were to cool down a little bit. But I am still here. I realise how fortunate that makes me – I have moved up in the world at just about the right pace, or at least close enough, to be able to stay put. But I am a Londoner, and this place is my home. When I read lazy stereotypes and criticisms of London and London-ers, I cannot help but take it personally.

All of which makes it very hard to write a calm, bal-anced response to this issue; I have attempted to do so nonetheless.

People and Place

Before we attempt to unravel the many different threads of historical and contemporary anti-London sentiment, we must first understand what 'London' and 'Londoners' really are. Both the city's people and the place itself are often stereotyped, misunderstood, and misrepresented, both wilfully and accidentally. While the reality is of course complex and multifaceted, a little more understanding about the capital itself – from its historical origins to its place in the UK economy today – is important. So, too, is an understanding of the much-maligned people who live there.

Londoners

At the start of 2020, before the coronavirus pandemic, London was home to nine million people, and this figure was expected only to increase. London's growth has been driven primarily by 'natural change' (births exceeding deaths), but also by new arrivals from overseas. In terms of domestic migration (that is, movement within the UK), more people tend to leave London for elsewhere in the country than arrive each year, with over half moving to the neighbouring south-east or east of England regions, often when reaching their thirties, perhaps to start families outside the city.[1] Somewhat relatedly, the average Londoner today is almost five years younger than the UK average, although the number of Londoners over the age of sixty-five is also increasing.[2]

Today's Londoners are also incredibly diverse, in every sense of the word. Over a third were born abroad, which is more than double the UK-wide proportion.[3] However, an estimated three-quarters are British citizens.[4] London's population is 41 per cent BME, which compares to 11 per cent nationally. However, the proportion of BME Londoners varies hugely by borough: from 13 per cent in Richmond upon Thames to 69 per cent in Brent.[5] London is also the most religiously diverse region of the UK.[6] One in five Londoners count a language other than English as their main language – this is closer to one in twenty in the rest of England and Wales[7] – and as many as 300 different languages are spoken by children in the capital's schools.[8] London looks, and sounds, different to the rest of the UK. But then, parts of London also look and sound entirely different to one another.

The capital's residents are quite at ease with their

differences, overall. Some evidence suggests that the capital's diverse communities mix slightly less than in other parts of the country.[9] But over three-quarters of Londoners report that people from different backgrounds get on well in their local area.[10] Almost one in twenty Londoners are of mixed ethnicity, and one in five London households contain people from different ethnic groups living together.[11] Residents of the UK capital generally identify most strongly as 'Londoners' ahead of being 'British' or 'English'.[12] This identity appears to be both inclusive and easily acquired; an increase in the percentage of Londoners who were born abroad has not reduced the strength of the London identity over several decades.[13] Of course, no city is perfect, and integration and inclusion require constant effort. But London's 'melting pot' is a remarkably successful one.

London's diversity does not mean that the average Londoner has more liberal views across the board, though. In fact, Londoners have more socially conservative views on average, regarding issues such as pre-marital sex and homosexuality, than their counterparts elsewhere in the UK. The fact that Londoners are more likely to identify as religious than the rest of Britain seems to go some way towards explaining this.[14] When religious affiliation is taken into account, these differences between London and other UK regions vanish.[15]

London not only looks and sounds different to the rest of the nation but it votes differently too. Over the last four decades, London has become an increasingly Labour-voting city, diverging further and further from England as a whole.[16] In 2016, it was also found to be a heavily 'remain' city, famously voting 60:40 in favour of staying in the EU while England as a whole voted to leave by 53:47 and the UK did the same by a slightly smaller margin. London is home to seven of the ten strongest remain-voting areas in the UK. But it is also true that five London boroughs voted leave, as did 40 per cent of all Londoners.[17] The capital also contains several safe Conservative seats and elected a Conservative mayor in two of five mayoral elections at the time of writing.

The capital is not a homogeneous place. Its residents are diverse, and many look and sound different to their counterparts elsewhere in the nation. To some extent, Londoners think and vote differently too. But the differences between Londoners and the rest of the UK can be exaggerated. Furthermore, Londoners are also different from one another, whether from borough to borough or community to community. Any claim that 'Londoners' think or act in a certain way requires several layers of caveating. Londoners tend to manage their differences with relative ease and feel a strong attachment to the city. But while some Londoners have arrived in the capital from elsewhere in the world, most are British citizens. Many are born and bred in the city; others come from elsewhere in the UK, and more still will live elsewhere in the UK in the future. In this sense, they are of the country as much as of the capital.

A global city

As well as being a place in its own right, London is the capital of both England and the UK. But it is also part of something global.

At the start of 2020, London was one of a handful of true 'world cities' on Earth. It fought for the top spot in various international city rankings, particularly those measuring the relative power of financial centres, the ability to attract the most mobile, highly skilled global talent and to draw foreign investment. In 2013, a 'Big Six' of global cities had pulled ahead of the rest: London, New York, Paris, Singapore, Tokyo, and Hong Kong. In 2016, Seoul joined a 'Big Seven'. London was not only firmly in this elite league but at its forefront: in 2019, it was ranked as the most economically competitive city in the world based on an analysis of indices of over 500 different criteria.[18]

London tended to fare somewhat less well in 'quality of life' rankings, not quite making the global top forty.[19] Yet its magnetism endured regardless. The new millennium had seen the UK capital's population and economy grow like Topsy. London's 'brand' was recognisable and respected worldwide, its economy dynamic and highly internationalised, and its population diverse. And while the UK's status as a welcoming and outward-looking place for talented migrants may have been diminished by the result of the EU referendum of June 2016, some evidence suggested that London's reputation for openness had endured, having decoupled from that of its nation.[20]

As 2020 began, the UK's capital was recognised around the world as a world-class place to do business, a cultural centre of great influence and 'soft power', and an international tourist destination thanks to a near-unique blend of 2,000 years of history and cutting-edge technology, ideas, and dynamism. Despite negative stereotypes earned over several hundred years, London had even begun to be seen as a good place to get a quality meal.[21]

The engine room of the UK economy

At home, London's economy was strong as it entered the 2020s – arguably too dominant, in fact, in the national context. While home to only 13 per cent of the UK population, the capital accounted for a quarter of the national economy.[22] Economic activity in London had stormed ahead of the UK average since the 1990s, with the gap between capital and country growing wider each year.[23] The UK capital was responsible for one-third of all taxes raised across the nation, more than the next thirty-seven biggest cities combined.[24] In 2017, Chris Giles observed in the *Financial Times* that 'if London [were] a nation state, it would have a budget surplus of 7 per cent of gross domestic product, better than Norway.'[25]

In other words, London's success helped pay for public services across the UK. The Greater London region had a sizeable 'fiscal surplus', contributing more in taxation to HM Treasury than it received in public spending. The only other two regions with fiscal surpluses were the neighbouring south-east and east of England regions, both of which have strong economic ties and substantial commuting patterns into the capital.[26] Together, these three regions create a combined 'wider south-east' mega-region of 24 million people, over a third of the UK's population.

In 2019, London had a net fiscal surplus of public spending per head of £4,369. Northern Ireland had a net *deficit* of £4,978 per head.[27] But this is not to single out Northern Ireland: outside the wider south-east, every other English region, plus Scotland and Wales, had net deficits. And London is undoubtedly the engine that drives the whole wider south-east mega-region: in 2018/19, London's total fiscal surplus stood at

£38.9 billion, compared to the south-east's £21.9 billion and the east of England's £4.2 billion.[28]

London's dominance of its nation is far from unique among global capitals. Cities like Tokyo and Seoul are home to a much larger share of their nation states' populations than London, while Moscow, Mumbai, and São Paulo are responsible for even greater shares of their national economies than London. Closer to home, the economic gap (in gross value added, GVA, per capita) between Paris and France is also larger.[29] But the London–UK gap remains cavernous: other UK cities lag notably behind London in terms of productivity. Of the twelve UK cities with more than 500,000 inhabitants in 2016, only three – London, Bristol, and Portsmouth – were more productive than the national average. In Germany, which is often lauded as a more successful 'multinodal' state, the comparable figure was nine out of fourteen. What's more, eight of these German cities perform better than the European average, whereas London is the only UK city to do so.[30]

It is a matter of fact, then, that London overperforms and other UK cities (and regions) underperform. Whether the former is responsible for the latter is much more debatable but, as this book will show, it is safe to say that the gap between London and the rest is desirable for neither capital nor country.

International magnet

London's global city status generates taxes that pay for public spending across the UK, but it also brings other benefits. It is the number one city in the world for foreign direct investment in headquarters for multinational corporations.[31] It draws investment worth billions into the UK that would otherwise go to one of the world's other great global hubs. In doing so, London competes with Singapore, Dubai, and Hong Kong – rather than Manchester, Birmingham, or Edinburgh. But that's not to say London alone reaps the benefits: aside from the national tax benefits that such investment generates, foreign direct investment in the capital also leads to spin-off investment elsewhere in the country. More than one in ten such projects outside London stemmed from an initial investment in the capital, generating billions and creating tens of thousands of jobs.[32]

Similarly, London's draw as an international tourist attraction has knock-on effects for the national economy. In 2019, Heathrow airport was the busiest in Europe, with over 80 million passengers passing through it.[33] London alone attracted 22 million overseas visitors, who spent nearly £16 billion in the UK;[34] 15 per cent of those went on to visit another UK location in the same trip.[35] London's universities also produce world-leading research, drawing over 100,000 international students into the capital each year.[36]

London's global magnetism brings positives for the entire country. But the capital's growth also depends on intra-UK trade. As successive mayors of London have pointed out, much of the capital's infrastructure is built or supplied by the rest of the UK.[37] London's leaders have sometimes expressed this hard economic truth in more or less tactful language, depending on sensitivities to the national feeling towards London, but the unvarnished truth is that the UK economy is (or, at least, was before the pandemic) dependent on London's success in several different ways.

Centre of everything?

This tremendous economic dynamism is fuelled in no small part by London's remarkable agglomeration of national and international functions: London – like Paris, Dublin, or Tokyo, but unlike Berlin, New York, or Rome – is the political, economic, and cultural focus of its nation. This convergence is not the fruit of deliberate, long-term planning but the result of a series of historical accidents, coincidences, and short-term decisions.

Roman Londinium, founded halfway into the first century AD, was a walled city of a similar size and location to what is today known as 'the City' or Square Mile. It was established on the banks of the River Thames, which connected the city to the world via the sea, and this connection would be crucial to London's development as a centre of world trade. Today that trade is in services not goods, but either way, the City of London has been a centre of economic power for almost 2,000 years.

A millennium after Londinium was founded, Edward the Confessor established Westminster as a seat of royal power with the construction of an abbey. Westminster, which lies a couple of miles to the west of the City, was separate from and named in geographical relation to London. As political power in the UK gradually transferred from hereditary monarchy to elected representatives, politicians too began to operate at Westminster.

The proximity of these two ancient cities – both home to raw power of differing natures, one political and the other economic – made their eventual unification almost inevitable. Inevitable too was the gradual and largely unplanned accretion of national functions in the ever-expanding metropolis that emerged between and around them.

In fact, as Chapter Two details, despite successive attempts to contain or control the capital's growth, even the greatest city planners – from Christopher Wren to Patrick Abercrombie – have been defeated by London's irrepressible, seemingly innate dynamism. Peter Rees, former chief planner at the City of London Corporation, branded London 'unplannable'.[38] Professor of town planning Michael Hebbert described the city as built 'more by fortune than design',[39] while LSE professor Tony Travers has called the modern capital 'ungovernable'.[40] London's growth has generally been organic and difficult to control – just like its outsized role within the nation.

If we were to start afresh, it seems unlikely that London would be selected as the UK's capital. Several comparable but younger nations deliberately chose and planned their capital cities, taking political and cultural considerations into account. Washington DC, for example, was selected expressly as a compromise between north and south. Australia built its capital, Canberra, at a point between its two largest cities, Melbourne and Sydney. Even so, debate on Canberra's exact location lasted for nine years; construction took a further seventeen.[41] Other nations have moved their capital cities for political reasons, but this has often proved expensive and disruptive and is rarely viewed as successful.[42]

London's historical position as both political and economic capital of the UK has given it an unstoppable momentum. Today, alongside central government, the nation's premier financial centre, and the monarchy, London is home to: the Royal Courts of Justice; the majority of the national print and broadcast media; the nation's busiest airport and railway station; national museums, galleries, and other major cultural institutions;

the largest national football, rugby, and cricket stadiums; the home stadiums of several of England's most successful local sports teams; eight Royal Parks; one point of the 'golden triangle' of the UK's top-ranking, world-leading universities (alongside Oxford and Cambridge); as well as numerous regulatory bodies, large business groups, and research institutions. It is a concentration of power of all kinds, with few parallels around the world.

National life

As a consequence, London is the focal point for moments of national importance. Royal weddings and national sporting victories are celebrated on the streets of Central London and broadcast across the UK. The entire country celebrated the end of the war in Europe in May 1945, but it was on Whitehall that the prime minister, Winston Churchill, addressed the assembled crowds. England's solitary football World Cup win in 1966 was celebrated modestly in the capital; the 2012 Olympics was a much more lavish moment of national jubilation. Its opening ceremony, a moving tribute to the UK's past and present, was hosted in a newly built stadium in east London. The last night of the Proms is an overtly patriotic British event, watched by millions but broadcast from the Royal Albert Hall in the capital.

Solemn moments, such as Remembrance Sunday, also

focus on London. Kings and queens are made at Westminster Abbey, where so many of the nation's significant political and military leaders, scientific innovators, and cultural icons are buried or commemorated. London is awash with statues and memorials to national figures once deemed worthy of posterity. And while the list of names and faces, alongside their reasons for being commemorated, is now rightly under review, the idea that the nation's greatest figures and finest ideas should be represented in its capital's public realm endures.

Equally, major protests see citizens travel from across the country to converge on the capital's public spaces, often in Trafalgar Square, Hyde Park, or Parliament Square. Here they gather to express opposition to issues as diverse as the Iraq War or the ban on foxhunting in the early 2000s or, more recently, to structural racism or the coronavirus lockdowns in 2020. Political power lies in the capital's streets as well as its historic buildings.

Regional imbalances?

With so much going on in one place, it is unsurprising that London has such a dominant role within its nation. The Institute for Fiscal Studies recently ranked the UK as one of the most geographically unequal nations in the developed world,[43] a notion that is often repeated.[44] London's dominance is far from ideal, for capital or country. The capital's gravitational pull fuels congestion and pollution as well as higher house prices in London itself, in addition to breeding resentment and draining talent from elsewhere in the UK. However, the story is of course more complex than it first appears.

London is a city, but its sheer size means that 'Greater London' is treated as a region. It is therefore compared to north-west England or the whole of Scotland rather than Manchester or Edinburgh. So while most commuters in other cities live (and therefore spend) in the same region in which they work, much of London's economic output is generated by commuters who live outside the Greater London region.[45] This makes London look richer than it is. Moreover, the units used to measure regional inequality are not consistent between nations and do not necessarily compare like with like.[46] The result is that, although the UK is certainly a regionally unequal place, the degree of inequality tends to be exaggerated.

Perhaps more important is the question of how we measure economic performance. Almost all such methods have their flaws. GVA per worker, generally accepted as one of the best ways to measure regional economic performance, still does not manage to factor in the relative purchasing power that results from such economic activity. Do those who work in highly productive regional economies have higher disposable incomes?

And if not, does this tell us much of anything about the experience of living and working in a particular part of the country?

We already know that London is the most productive region of the UK.[47] But although London's economic output continued to pull ahead of the national average after the financial crisis of 2007–8, this lead was not matched by a rise in productivity per hour worked; instead, the rise was down to a growth in (mainly low-paid) employment. All the while, the 'London premium' of higher wages offsetting higher living costs has been reducing, as the growth of the latter outstrips that of the former.[48] Londoners are therefore working harder and longer, for less and less reward, compared with the rest of the country. GVA measurements tell us what we already know: regional imbalances are an issue in the UK. But what does a 'higher' GVA mean for Londoners if their money doesn't stretch as far as that of their compatriots elsewhere in the UK?

London imbalances
The economic strength of the Greater London region does not mean that life is wonderful for all of its residents. Londoners are more likely than the average Brit to say they wish they had more free time – unsurprising given they also spend more of their time at work.[49] With

the longest average commute times in the country, Londoners also face some of the nation's most overcrowded trains.[50] Office for National Statistics annual personal well-being estimates find that Londoners are less likely to describe themselves as 'happy' than the national average; they are also least likely to feel their life is 'worthwhile'. Added to that, Londoners report the lowest overall life satisfaction and the highest rates of anxiety.[51] Suffice it to say, life in the capital in early 2020 was no easy ride.

London's wealth is not shared evenly between its residents. While the gap between London and the rest of the country is sizeable, as the Institute for Fiscal Studies noted, 'inequalities within regions are larger than the inequalities between regions.'[52] There is a yawning gap between the opportunities, economic outcomes, and life experiences of the poorest and richest Londoners. In fact, the capital has the greatest wealth inequality in the UK, and this divide has grown over the last decade.[53] As the think tank the Smith Institute observed in 2015, 'London is a strange, complicated, contradictory place ... as if a large, poor town cohabited uneasily with a large, rich town.'[54]

This 'large, poor town' is often forgotten. In the first part of 2020, 28 per cent of Londoners (2.5 million people) were living in poverty; across England the figure was 22 per cent. Poverty rates in the capital have exceeded the national average for over twenty years, and over the last five years both the number and proportion of Londoners living in poverty have increased.[55] Shamefully, London is the region with the highest level of child poverty in the UK, by some distance, and it is forecast to remain as such.[56]

There is also great inequality among London's poor. The poverty rate for BME Londoners is almost twice that of white Londoners.[57] Life expectancy, health outcomes, and infant mortality rates vary substantially between boroughs.[58] In a very telling statistic, each stop eastwards on the Jubilee Line from Westminster represents nearly a year off the life expectancy of those who live nearby.[59] Housing costs are an especially potent part of the mix. Once they are factored in, Londoners' average incomes are in line with the rest of the UK, eradicating any 'London premium' in pay; in fact, poorer Londoners are left worse off than their counterparts elsewhere.[60] Meanwhile, incomes for working-age Londoners have stagnated since the early 2000s.[61] The capital's streets are far from paved with gold – or, rather, a very small number are, and not everyone is welcome to walk them.

The route out of poverty in London is full of obstacles – housing costs and the prevalence of low-paid work being two examples, as already mentioned. But the route does exist. London provides opportunities to 'move up' in the world that are simply not available to those in more remote parts of the country. Children on free school meals in London achieve a higher rate of A* to C grades at GCSE than those in other regions, and London accounted for nearly two-thirds of the nation's social mobility 'hotspots' as identified by the Social Mobility Commission in 2017.[62]

Londoners are also generally more likely to have a higher level of qualification to their name than the average Brit.[63] Some of this is the result of a strong educational offering for the capital's young people, but some is the result of educated people moving to live there. At the start of 2020, the Sutton Trust noted that moving to London in your early-to-mid thirties to work in an elite occupation is 'overwhelmingly associated with being from a privileged background ... "ordinary" Londoners who move into elite occupations actually tend to move away from London in order to accomplish their ascent.'[64] In other words, 'the Dick Whittington vision of moving to the capital to move up in the world is largely a myth.'[65] So while there is opportunity in the city, it tends to be the most privileged who have the resources and the facilities to capitalise on it.

London, Londoners, and the UK

London is an unequal place in its own right, then. But, as already alluded to, stark, sizeable differences in productivity, economic activity, and employment also exist between London and the rest of the UK. This has often led to the accusation that poor economic performance elsewhere in the country is the result of, or in some way connected to, London's success.[66] Many other world cities face the same criticisms, particularly those in non-federal nations, but the imbalance of London and the UK has its own idiosyncrasies and a very long history, as Chapter Two demonstrates.

London plays a crucial role in the UK economy, houses a highly centralised national government, and serves as a cultural centre of national life. It is the place where the nation comes to celebrate and to protest. Indeed, its role in the UK is arguably outsized. Its residents, however, do not necessarily feel the benefit of the capital's supposed success. They vote, look, and sound different to the rest of the nation, furthering a sense of divergence between capital and country, even if this difference can be overstated. Perhaps this explains why the national conversation has, in recent years, turned increasingly towards the inequalities between London and the rest of the UK rather than the inequalities between Londoners themselves. But how did we get here?

2

Politics and Policy

The relationship between London and the rest of its nation has been a challenging one for almost as long as there has been a London. In recent years, relations seem to have taken a turn for the worse. But while some of the causes of this antagonism are particular to our times, and some are indeed entirely novel, others are longstanding grievances that have now become acute. This chapter puts the issues of today in context by providing a short history of London's relationship with the nation.

In September 2014, as mayor of London, Boris Johnson said, 'A pound invested in London can drive jobs and growth around the country ... When London grows the rest of the country grows.'[1] Chapter One has shown that there is truth in this claim. In June 2020, as prime minister, Boris Johnson observed that 'too many parts of this country have felt left behind, neglected, unloved, as though someone had taken a strategic decision that their fate did not matter as much as the metropolis.'[2] The historical reality of this claim is examined in this chapter. Chapter Three goes on to examine the wider public 'feeling' towards London.

'Levelling up'

Boris Johnson is the first former mayor of London to become prime minister of the United Kingdom. His government was elected in 2019 on a commitment to 'level up' the UK, a carefully chosen phrase that suggests tackling regional inequalities by boosting the economy and improving opportunities outside of London and the south-east rather than attacking or 'levelling down' the capital.

The 2019 general election was notable for its results across the newly named 'red wall', a former Labour stronghold of constituencies stretching from north Wales to the north-east of England. Much of the red wall voted Conservative in 2019, in many cases for the first time.[3] Alongside the pledge to 'get Brexit done', Johnson's Conservative manifesto targeted these voters with a promise to 'level up' the nation by completing major infrastructure projects outside the capital, particularly in transport, renewing commitment to concepts such as the Northern Powerhouse and Midlands Engine, and delivering 'full devolution across England'.[4]

The promise to 'level up' was an escalation of an

existing commitment by Theresa May's Conservative Party, whose 2017 manifesto promised to build:

> A stronger economy that works for everyone – where wealth and opportunity are spread across every community in the United Kingdom, not just the most prosperous places in London and the south east.[5]

This, in turn, followed the 2015 Conservative Party manifesto, which committed to 'rebalance our economy and build a Northern Powerhouse'.[6]

Whether this ambition to combat the UK's regional inequalities has been fulfilled is yet to be seen, but it is important to note that 'levelling up' does not exist in a vacuum. It has a wider context – historical, political, and cultural. As the Institute for Fiscal Studies has noted, regional inequalities in the UK are 'deep-rooted and complex', and so any 'levelling up' needs to be 'a long-term, multifaceted agenda if it is to succeed where other governments have failed in the past'.[7] And many have failed. The UK's 'London problem' is not a sudden illness but a chronic condition, one that flares up periodically throughout the nation's history.

A history of London 'problems'
London's seemingly uncontrollable growth has been

considered a problem for hundreds of years. Elizabeth I issued a royal proclamation in 1580, followed by an Act of Parliament in 1592 which effectively placed an early version of a 'green belt' around London in an attempt to stall its growth.[8] It met with little success. At the start of the seventeenth century, as London swelled ever further outside the walls of the original Roman city, James I mournfully observed that 'soon, London will be all England.'[9]

Over centuries, London has faced several devastating fires, outbreaks of plague, and numerous other epidemics. Even the Industrial Revolution posed a threat to the capital in that it boosted other UK cities and almost passed London by. But London survived them all, somehow continuing to acquire more national significance and more people, and generating ever more activity. In 1783, the economist Josiah Tucker noted that London had first been 'looked upon to be no better than a Wen, or Excrescence, in the Body Politick' 200 years prior. It had only grown since.[10] He wondered if 'this overgrown metropolis ought not to be stripped of its borrowed Greatness, and be reduced to its primitive and just Mediocrity?'[11] Tucker's was an eighteenth-century proposal to move parliament out of London, in this case to Edinburgh. Similar proposals would be made repeatedly for hundreds of years thereafter, never to be fulfilled.

The next century saw London's growth explode. The capital entered the 1800s surpassing one million residents, becoming the largest city in western Europe since Rome's peak. By 1840, it had two million and was the largest city in the history of the world, and by the end of the 1800s, London was home to over six million people.[12] This represented a jump from 12 per cent of the population of England and Wales at the start of the nineteenth century to over 20 per cent by the century's close.[13] This growth was driven almost entirely by the migration of English, Welsh, and Scottish people, contributing to the sense that London's expansion came at the expense of the rest of the nation.[14] Indeed, it was in 1822 that William Cobbett famously labelled London 'the Great Wen', and towards the end of the 1800s, the Liberal chairman of the London County Council Lord Rosebery would wonder at the 'awfulness' of the capital: 'If it was a wen then what is it now? A tumour, an elephantiasis sucking into its gorged system half the life and blood and the bone of the rural districts.'[15]

It wasn't until the 1930s that a proper 'green belt' finally began to be drawn around London, placing an outward limit on the capital's future expansion. But its population continued to swell. By 1939, there were 8.6 million Londoners, the largest population the capital had ever seen. A weak national economy only saw greater numbers migrate to London in search of work, and so while the nation endured economic depression, London grew. As historian Jerry White described it, 'many put two and two together and concluded that London was sucking the vitality from the nation's very bloodstream, like some gluttonous parasite.'[16]

The interwar years had seen the UK government try different approaches to addressing regional imbalances. First, an Industrial Transference Board was established in 1928 to encourage the unemployed in struggling industrial areas to relocate to areas with jobs and training schemes – generally in London and the south-east.[17] Then, the Special Areas Act of 1934 sought to 'take work to the workers', enabling the government to construct industrial premises and provide direct grants to the struggling regions in an attempt to stimulate economic growth.[18] This second approach laid the groundwork for a post-war consensus in regional policy that would last for decades.

London and the war
The Second World War changed a great deal for London. Heavy bombing killed and injured citizens and flattened the capital's buildings, while evacuation saw Londoners deliberately moved elsewhere. What's more, two wartime inquiries actively encouraged the depopulation

of the capital in the years after the war: the Barlow Commission on the 'Distribution of the Industrial Population', which reported in 1940, and Patrick Abercrombie's 1943/1944 plans for the County of London and Greater London. The inquiries diagnosed different ailments and, in some ways, offered different cures, but both resulted in a broadly anti-London consensus that saw the capital's population – and its economy – decline for decades.

Barlow urged the decentralisation of industry from the UK's major urban areas, both to assist struggling regional economies and to improve the nation's 'sprawling, ill-planned, chaotic, and congested' cities.[19] Abercrombie's plans for London also encouraged 'the removal of an appreciable amount of industry and commerce from Central London' to enable reconstruction.[20] But Abercrombie also promoted the 'decentralisation' of Londoners themselves: over a million people were to be encouraged out of crowded, polluted, and slum-ridden Inner London and into cleaner, greener, and more spacious new towns, garden cities, and suburbs.[21]

The Distribution of Industry Act 1945, described as the 'foundation of British regional policy', then took up Barlow's cause.[22] Subsequent post-war consensus on regional policy was dominated by what Jerry White calls the 'London-as-problem paradigm'.[23] Successive governments placed limits on economic activity in London, constraining the construction of, firstly, factories and, later, offices. The 1963 legislation that established the Greater London Council (GLC) contained a clause that made it illegal to advertise industrial opportunities in London.[24] New office development in Central London was effectively banned by Labour's George Brown in 1964, albeit temporarily.[25] Meanwhile, governments intervened to incentivise, subsidise, and sometimes construct factories elsewhere in the country. Investment was pushed out of the city and towards the suburbs in the ultimately frustrated hope that it might reach the rest of the country. In the most part, the furthest that new factories and offices were dispersed was Outer London and the south-east. All the while, London declined – and the UK economy did the same.

Consensus over?

Margaret Thatcher's election in 1979 saw an end to this post-war consensus, as previewed in the Conservative manifesto: 'Strategies and plans cannot produce revival, nor can subsidies.'[26] Displacing jobs to 'inefficient' areas was seen as unwise, and funding for regional development was reduced.[27] Instead, the Thatcher government shifted from a 'regional' to a 'local' approach to changing the fortunes of declining areas.[28]

Thatcher was no great lover of London. The 'Big

Bang' of City deregulation on 27 October 1986 – which dramatically revitalised London's financial sector – was heavily associated with Thatcherism, but in reality it was largely the result of a process begun under Harold Wilson's Labour government. Thatcher personally found the stock exchange quite distasteful.[29] As prime minister, she also famously abolished the GLC, irritated by its left-wing leader Ken Livingstone, leaving the capital without city-wide government for the first time in the twentieth century.

Yet the Thatcher years saw regional inequalities widen substantially, with London and the south-east of England the benefactors. The cause was rapid deindustrialisation, particularly outside the south-east, alongside the boom of an increasingly internationalised, mainly services-based economy focused in the capital. London's economy soared away from the rest of the nation once more. The Big Bang corresponded roughly with the point at which the capital's population began to grow again, following decades of decline. By 1990, regional inequalities had started to reopen significantly.[30]

New Labour, elected in 1997, did not implement a full return to the post-war consensus but took a 'third way' approach. London-wide government was restored from 2000, recast into a mayoral model in an attempt to avoid recreating the controversial GLC. So-called regional development agencies were introduced from 1998 across the country, including in London, to encourage and enable local economic development. As the UK economy entered a decade of growth, investment was driven back up and channelled through the regional development agencies.[31] London and the south-east continued to grow, but the rising tide of prosperity appeared to be genuinely lifting all boats.

In 2006, the chancellor of the Exchequer, Gordon Brown, cited London (meaning the City) as a shining example to the nation: 'The message London's success sends out to the whole British economy is that we will succeed if like London we think globally.'[32] The following June, he told the City: 'Britain needs more of the vigour, ingenuity, and aspiration that you already demonstrate is the hallmark of your success.'[33] New Labour's regional policy did much good, with several of the regional development agencies proving particularly successful, but the gap between the north and south of England remained.[34] And the decade-long wave of economic growth that the nation had been riding was about to crash.

Crash and coalition

Just months after Brown's second speech, the run on Northern Rock began, the first major manifestation of the global financial crash of 2007–8 in the UK. The crash had a huge and direct effect on relations between the capital and the rest of the nation. As historian Peter Mandler noted, 'bankers and politicians were blamed ... but the rest of the country paid the price.'[35] The capital – the home of both groups – bore the brunt of the criticism, but London's 'guilty' did not appear to suffer the consequences. What's more, the capital came through the crash with its economy relatively unharmed. Some argue that this was the result of deliberate policy choices made by central government coming to the aid of the nation's mostly London-based financial services with 'implicit subsidies', bailouts, and monetary expansion through quantitative easing and bank rate reductions.[36]

Shortly afterwards, in 2009, the MPs' expenses scandal further undermined trust in the occupants of London's other ancient city: Westminster. None of this was the fault of the average Londoner, of course, but a mounting anti-establishment feeling was beginning to find its geographical focus in the capital. Not only was the economy still skewed southwards despite decades of discussion and policy announcements, but those considered responsible appeared to be getting away scot-free. As of 2019, politician and banker remained among the least trusted professions in the UK.[37]

The Conservative–Liberal Democrat coalition government was elected in 2010, with the senior partners committed to substantial cuts in order to balance the UK's books.[38] The rest of the UK (and, though less often acknowledged, the rest of London outside SW1 and the Square Mile) would suffer the consequences of the crash through years of austerity, substantial cuts to public services, and stagnant wages. Ten years post-crash, we saw that London's councils actually bore a disproportionate share of the cuts in public expenditure that followed.[39] But the cuts hit the entire country, and as London's economy continued to grow, leaving the rest of the nation behind, it certainly didn't look like London was being punished.

Academics have explicitly linked the effects of the financial crash to the new prominence of policies and political rhetoric around 'rebalancing the economy'.[40] Contrast, for instance, Gordon Brown's praise for London's financial services sector in 2006 with, just four years later, Conservative prime minister David Cameron's declaration that 'today our economy is heavily reliant on just a few industries and a few regions – particularly London and the South East ... we are determined that should change.'[41]

Despite the rhetorical shift, the coalition government's attempts to address the UK's geographic imbalances were delivered on the cheap. Regional policy (now rebranded as 'rebalancing' the economy) shifted back towards the 'local'. Spending was reduced once more, and the Localism Act of 2011 saw thirty-nine smaller 'local enterprise partnerships', which brought the private sector into local decision-making, replace eight large regional development agencies at a fraction of the cost.

Deregulatory 'Enterprise Zones' were introduced in designated localities across the country, and so-called City Deals provided funding to some, but not all, cities. Combined authority (or 'metro') mayors were established to give city regions outside London a focal point for local leadership in the hope that this could lead to stronger regional growth. Initiatives such as the Northern Powerhouse and the Midlands Engine were easily criticised as gimmicky but have delivered leadership alongside some investment, as well as providing identifiable regional brands for foreign investors.[42] But much like the 'Big Society', a phrase David Cameron promoted to encourage volunteering and community initiatives during his premiership, it was easy to view the coalition's austerity-hampered commitment to 'rebalancing' as mainly rhetorical.

All the while, regional resentments continued to grow. The populist United Kingdom Independence Party (UKIP) was now on the rise, particularly in the east of England. Journalist John Harris travelled the country conducting interviews for a series entitled 'Anywhere but Westminster'. In September 2014, the *Guardian* published an editorial, reporting:

> ... a geographical animus. The symbol of most ills is seen to be London ... Westminster represents the infection at its most extreme, but the animosity transcends politics. It focuses on London as a city state, with a different way of life, a different culture.[43]

A national climate of austerity, albeit one in which the economic gap between the capital and the rest continued to grow, does not quite explain these sentiments. They certainly played a part, but they belie a broader cultural disconnect, leading to growing anti-establishment sentiments. That same month, a divisive referendum campaign culminated in Scotland deciding to remain part of the United Kingdom – but by a tighter-than-expected margin. The UK was becoming an increasingly divided place.

EU referendum

In 2015, Cameron's Conservatives were re-elected with a majority on a pledge to hold a referendum on the UK's membership of the EU. Then, on 23 June 2016, the UK voted to leave by a margin of 51.9 per cent to 48.1 per cent. The motivations behind this binary decision on the part of the nation's voters were complex and numerous. It has been argued that they include opposition to immigration and multiculturalism, globalisation, deindustrialisation, austerity, the 'establishment', and an overly centralised British state. Meanwhile, the geographical spread of votes across the UK has been seen as demonstrating a growing urban–rural divide, a north–south divide, big cities versus 'left-behind' post-industrial and coastal towns, a growing cultural chasm between a London-based 'elite' and the rest of the country, and an area's proportion of voters with a university-level education. Genuine opposition to the UK's membership of the EU, or a sense that the EU was too remote and distant and therefore an undesirable form of government, was a less widely discussed possible motivation.

What was clear was that the referendum revealed a divided nation. In its most extreme manifestation, the MP Jo Cox was murdered in broad daylight in the build-up to the vote by a man reportedly shouting 'Britain first'. The souring of political discourse continued post-referendum and has now lasted for several years. As previously mentioned, London voted the opposite way to England and the UK as a whole. Other big English cities also voted to remain, as did Scotland and Northern Ireland, but while London is treated as a region, compared to Scotland or the north-east for example, other cities found their remain-voting tendencies diluted and left relatively unnoticed within their wider leave-voting regions. Ultimately, the referendum highlighted already notable differences between capital and country. None of the many previously mentioned different fractures in the unity of the UK began with the EU referendum, but the debate leading up to (and following) it, as well as the binary nature of the choice itself, certainly pushed them to the fore, increasing the national focus on what divides us, and giving these divisions new referendum-related labels and logos to rally around.

One side of the debate certainly did not like London. In 2014, UKIP councillor Suzanne Evans blamed her party's poor local election performance in London on the capital's 'more media-savvy and educated' population, who were more likely to have read and believed negative press about UKIP.[44] Earlier that year, UKIP leader Nigel Farage had described how he 'felt awkward' on a train out of Central London, where 'it wasn't until after we got past Grove Park that I could actually hear English being audibly spoken in the carriage'.[45] In John Harris's words, Farage's party was 'an anti-metropolitan revolt rooted in parts of southern and eastern England that often feel peripheral relative to London.'[46]

And London did not necessarily like the other side much either. The aftermath of the results saw several articles published in national media outlets jokingly proposing independence for London.[47] A tongue-in-cheek petition for 'Londependence' garnered over 180,000 signatures.[48] Between October 2014 and July 2016, support for London independence more than doubled in the capital – albeit from a low one in twenty to a still relatively low one in ten Londoners.[49] In 2017, the MP David Lammy called for 'a well-overdue debate about London becoming more autonomous and independent', explaining that 'the case for a London city-state has never been stronger.'[50]

The EU referendum was a flash of lightning that illuminated a wider landscape of discontent. And that lightning also set a few fires going. Subsequent years saw anti-Londonism voiced increasingly regularly, broadly, and angrily. Political manifestos began to dedicate more space to addressing the gap between London and the rest of the country, and there was a broader backlash against 'elites' and 'experts' – considered 'metropolitan' or 'liberal' in their nature – that operated alongside efforts to rebalance the UK economy. The debate was no longer about the location of factories or civil servants but a multifaceted clash over identity, representation, democracy, and culture.

The May government

In 2017, Theresa May's Conservative Party pledged to develop a 'modern industrial strategy' to rebalance the economy away from London, redirect arts funding elsewhere, and move civil servants (and Channel Four) out of the capital.[51] This was, in part, a response to sentiments expressed in, and arguably amplified by, the EU referendum in 2016 but, much like the numerous reasons for the vote itself, anti-London feeling was by then refracted through the prism of Brexit into many different shades.

One shade focused on regional investment in transport infrastructure. In early 2018, the think tank IPPR North claimed that London was set to receive 2.6 times as much infrastructure investment from central government as the north of England over the next five years.[52] HM Treasury, however, claimed that the south was actually due to receive less than the north. Both claims had truth to them, but they used different methodologies to produce the results that they wished to present.[53] A period of chaos and cancellations on the railways in May 2018 made things worse, as did what some perceived to be London-centric coverage by national media.[54]

Public transport provision outside of London had unquestionably suffered from a lack of investment over the previous decades, so it's understandable that London's shiny new infrastructure generated resentment elsewhere in the country. However, national government was already beginning to 'rebalance' planned investment away from the capital. Additionally, Londoners alone were paying for more and more of the capital's infrastructure – arguably unfairly, given that they also pay for investment in the rest of the country, and commuters across the wider south-east regularly use London's transport without being asked to contribute towards its construction. As of March 2018, Transport for London no longer receives a central government grant towards its operating costs. Crossrail was part-funded by an additional tax on London-based businesses, and over half of the planned 'Crossrail 2' would be funded by London-only sources.[55] Nevertheless, the idea that London received 'more than its fair share' persisted.

Away from transport, other new pots of funding were established to counter the idea that London 'gets everything'. A 'Stronger Towns' fund, initiated under May but ultimately delivered by her successor, Boris Johnson, was established to provide funding to 'left behind' towns across the country. The allocation of such funding, however, has proved highly controversial: the criteria have been unclear and subject to accusations of politicisation.[56] And the politics were increasingly volatile. In November 2017, mayor of London Sadiq Khan attacked 'the most anti-London Budget in a generation' for its affordable housing funding pledges; earlier that year, he had branded May 'the most anti-London leader of a mainstream party since Margaret Thatcher.'[57]

Some of this was about more than just funding. May's 2016 Conservative Party Conference speech claimed that 'if you believe you're a citizen of the world, you're a citizen of nowhere.' This may have been aimed at bosses who undervalue workers, or international companies who don't pay their taxes, but the phrase echoed wider populist criticisms of an internationalised, metropolitan 'elite' widely associated with the capital.[58] The phrase also paid tribute to the anti-internationalist sentiments expressed by elements of the Leave campaign. The following week, the *Daily Mail* praised May for fighting for the Brexit cause against 'a well-heeled group of London "intellectuals" which is used to having everything its own way', a group that included anyone from the BBC to prominent politicians.[59]

Six months later, May announced a general election, at which she lost her majority. The prime minister resigned on 7 June 2019, having repeatedly failed to get her Brexit deal through parliament. Her successor, the darling of the Leave campaign, was to be an Old Etonian former mayor of London and resident of Islington.

The Johnson administration

The Johnson government's 'levelling up' agenda has been heavily focused on funding new transport projects, alongside electrification and 'smart ticketing'. Before the coronavirus pandemic hit, the government pledged to invest £100 billion in infrastructure.[60] Some questioned this emphasis on transport, arguing that regions need better skills provision, housing, or commercial space, alongside stronger local governance with more devolved powers,[61] but the sums discussed were undoubtedly impressive.

Despite these promises, Johnson's administration also saw an escalation of political tensions between London-wide and national government even prior to the pandemic. In March 2020, the government blocked the mayor of London's 'London Plan', the spatial plan for the city and one of the mayor's key responsibilities. Its response not only proposed a number of changes but, as Tony Travers has observed, was 'unapologetically critical' of the plan and, in a broader sense, 'dismissive of the mayor and his use of his powers'.[62] And that's to say nothing of the pandemic's impact on Transport for London's finances – a source of even more difficulty for relations between London-wide and central government – which is explored later.

Some of this is simple politics, of course, but there is also a bigger battle between a national government dominated by leave-supporting Conservatives and the remain-supporting mayor of a remain-supporting capital. Enduring policies, such as the relocation of civil servants away from Whitehall, are now described using rhetoric reminiscent of the Leave campaign, with a 'broken' civil service criticised for suffering from a lack of 'diversity of geography and cognition', led by a majority of 'urban metropolitan thinkers'.[63] The chancellor of the Duchy of Lancaster, Michael Gove, claimed that 'government departments recruit in their own image, and are influenced by the think-tanks and lobbyists who breathe the same London air and are socially rooted in assumptions which are inescapably metropolitan.'[64]

For Gove, London's air was not only polluted but it was imbued with a certain set of values and metropolitan assumptions that, once inhaled, left Londoners unable to understand or empathise with their counterparts elsewhere in the country. The idea of moving the House of Lords to York was repeatedly floated by the same government, albeit with a slightly different rationale.[65] It seems highly unlikely that this will happen, but the symbolism is what counts here: it has consistently been more appealing to central government to consider moving those aspects of central government that they feel least crucial out of London than to seriously consider devolving serious power to a local level, another perennial promise.

Centuries of rebalancing

Regional imbalance is one of many issues with which the UK has wrestled for decades but to which it has been unable to settle on an approach, let alone a solution. In 2017, Peter Hennessy calculated that the May government's 'Industrial Strategy' was the ninth such strategy proposed in his lifetime.[66] Hennessy returned to the theme in the House of Lords in January 2018:

> My Lords, why has it proved so tough for successive Governments to shape a successful industrial strategy that inspires, bites and, above all, endures? It is as if the framers of such strategies have been so many sculptors gazing at a rough-hewn piece of marble and discerning in it the outline of a beautifully cut statue, there for the crafting, but the resulting piece of work never quite fulfils the hopes of those who created it.[67]

The same could surely be said for the closely related area of regional policy.

After hundreds of years of attempting to adjust the balance of the nation, and particularly its economy, away from London and the south-east of England, what has actually been achieved? Surprisingly little. Ultimately, by the start of the twenty-first century, regional inequality did not look much different to the way it did at the start of the twentieth. In between, both London and the UK had declined economically.[68] It has been argued that London's dominance of the national economy tends to increase in periods of globalisation, and these also tend to be periods in which the entire national economy does well in comparison to other nations or historical trends.[69] This appears to be true. However, the idea that economic growth is a zero-sum game, with London required to 'lose' for others to gain, or that growth in London has a direct and inverse effect on growth in the rest of the country, has much less of a clear basis.[70]

While the nature of the national (and global) economy has changed over hundreds of years, the highly centralised nature of the UK's political system has not. This stasis surely plays some role in making London's dominance a continuing, recurring problem. The UK is among the most centralised nations in the OECD countries in terms of revenues raised, retained, and spent at a sub-national level.[71] Federal states appear less likely to have one dominant city; Germany and the USA are obvious examples. Decentralised nation states also tend to have a smaller gap between the size of their largest city and the next largest city. Even among unitary states, this gap in the UK is still over 1.5 times the average.[72]

Whatever the cause, the gap between London and the

rest of the UK is yet to be meaningfully addressed. As Ron Martin and his colleagues described in 2016:

> Despite nearly 90 years of regional policy interventions, substantial regional disparities in economic prosperity remain, and have in fact widened to reach levels not seen since the inter-war years. Past efforts to achieve a more spatially balanced distribution of economic activity and economic growth have failed to have any substantial or lasting impact.[73]

Today's 'levelling up' agenda has an important and admirable aim, but to achieve its goals it must succeed where so many of its predecessors have failed.

Rising anti-establishment, anti-elite, anti-city-dweller, and anti-internationalist sentiments, however, are more novel – or at least more recent. Much of this 'anti' feeling has been misdirected onto the capital and, by extension, its residents. Not only has this sentiment damaged the cohesion of the country but, as historian David Edgerton has observed, it has ironically been almost exclusively orchestrated by individuals of unquestionably elite backgrounds and lifestyles, often themselves based in the capital.[74]

In this way, the rise of populism has provided a megaphone for grievance, but little by way of solutions.

Populism, anti-immigration, and anti-globalisation sentiments are not the same as regional policy, by any means, but the latter is increasingly described using the language of the former. And all the while, the tone of the national conversation is becoming more unpleasant. What impact does all this have? Well, a less 'united' kingdom is less likely to come up with solutions and more likely to thrash out in rage. The following chapter looks at how this division manifests itself in widespread public misunderstandings across the country today.

3

Perceptions and Prejudices

Today's 'London-as-problem' paradigm is much more multifaceted and complex than the primarily economic concerns of the initial post-war decades. In early 2020, the *Times* published a comment piece which captured some of the newer elements of contemporary anti-London sentiment. First, a form of cultural disconnect:

> London, in its echo chamber, doesn't really get it ... Many of us beyond the North Circular do not like what the writer John Gray calls the 'hyper-liberalism' of the capital's institutions being imposed upon the rest of us. We resent the obsession with identity politics and the imposition of a secular, right-on 'wokeness', visible every day on the BBC, within the Labour Party and even in the Tory party.[1]

London, in this case, is portrayed as the physical headquarters of a set of cultural values, the epicentre of a liberal ideology that is both disconnected from the reality of life elsewhere in the country, and imposed upon it from the capital. In addition, London's supposed liberalism is perceived as something that it says rather than does: the piece goes on to cite the tragic fire at Grenfell Tower as evidence that London is 'an exploitative city state', good for its affluent white population but terrible for its ethnic minorities: 'A kind of ultra-secular Dubai, then ... We think London is kidding itself.'[2]

David Goodhart's *The Road to Somewhere* combines these threads in a more academic fashion, describing London as 'Anywhereville' and critiquing 'the London conceit'.[3] For Goodhart, the UK capital is a transient, rootless place, reliant on constant exploitative immigration, which is deeply unhappy and unequal. According to him, London is also a self-deluded city, with its own hypocritical ideology emphasising the social values of the 'new left' over the economics of the 'old left' (which Goodhart describes as 'Doreen Lawrence rather than the late Bob Crow'), and it 'simply ignores what does not fit its worldview'.[4]

London is all these things – and it is the complete opposite as well. The capital's name clearly means very different things to different people. For some, 'London' means modern capitalism, globalisation, raw power, and big money. Economist Paul Collier wrote in 2018 that the rest of the UK needed to be 'saved' from the capital: 'London is not shackled to a corpse; the rest of the country is shackled to a shark.'[5] Historians Peter Mandler and David Edgerton both argued separately that Brexit was the result of misplaced anger at 'London' (by which they mean an economy over-reliant on financial services) being redirected towards the EU.[6]

For other commentators, 'London' means national government based in Westminster and Whitehall, and decisions made centrally by remote and abstracted power structures. One leader of a northern city council described London to me as 'a place, but it's also a code word for a lot of things – parliament, judiciary, the media... it's code for, in effect, the pillars of our state.'[7] Regional politicians and commentators alike have repeatedly criticised national government as 'London-centric' in recent years; this criticism has only become more prevalent in response to the regional approach to the coronavirus pandemic in 2020.

For others, 'London' can mean the national media. In early 2019, journalist Helen Pidd observed that 'too many people who are making the news, and reporting on the news, live in London, and that really affects your world view. Sometimes it really does feel like a different country down there.'[8] The idea that London-based institutions dominate national life is widespread, particularly in the arena of politics and policymaking but also in the national conversations that inform these processes.

But the above examples are ultimately the views of journalists, historians, and politicians; they merely represent versions of opinions held more widely among sections of the British public. This chapter investigates these popular beliefs in more detail.

What do we mean by 'London'?

Polling undertaken by YouGov in June 2018 found that while 45 per cent of Britons had a favourable opinion of the capital, 28 per cent had an unfavourable view. The north of England, Scotland, and Wales were the most anti-London parts of the United Kingdom.[9] Broad anti-Londonism was a minority position in the nation at large, then, but it was still a sizeable one. Which 'London' are they talking about – and is the 'London' they describe real or imagined?

In 2018, Centre for London asked Brits outside the capital which of London's many different functions they thought of first when they heard the city's name. The top answer, by some margin, was, 'the home of Parliament and the UK's central government'.[10] So when newspaper headlines use 'London' to mean 'UK central government', perhaps they are simply reflecting a commonly held conflation between the two.[11] This tendency has been exacerbated in the national media in the context of the Brexit negotiations, with 'London' and 'Brussels' repeatedly used as shorthand for the UK and EU negotiating teams.[12]

It does not help that national government is so centralised. A 2014 poll by Survation found that two-thirds of adults across the UK agree that 'too much of England is run from London'.[13] The same year, polling by the Centre for Cities and Centre for London found that only 17 per cent of UK adults living in cities other than London felt parliament and Whitehall were responsive to local issues where they lived.[14] Local government and local politicians are significantly more trusted to deliver services than national government and MPs.[15] But with the majority of decisions taken centrally in today's UK, frustrations with national government are passed on to 'London'; in other words, it is guilty by association.

'Golden goose'?

Surely Brits at least like the wealth that the capital generates? To some extent, they do. In 2019, Centre for London found that 77 per cent of Britons outside of London felt that London contributed 'a lot' or 'a fair amount' to the national economy. This was up from 66 per cent in 2014. However, just 16 per cent felt that London contributed to 'the economy of the city/town/area where I live'; this compares to 24 per cent in 2014.[16]

So while Brits recognise that London contributes to the national purse in an abstract sense, there is a disconnect between this theoretical concept and what they see and feel locally. Combine this with the widespread feeling that the capital's financial services-dominated economy was both responsible for the crash and unfairly bailed out in the years that followed while the nation as a whole endured a harsh period of austerity, and it is understandable that the capital is unpopular.

Economic and political concerns also intertwine. There is a widespread perception that London receives 'more than its fair share' of central government investment because the politicians and civil servants who make investment decisions live and work in the capital. In 2019, YouGov found 60 per cent of Brits felt London 'gets more than its fair share' of public spending. This increased with physical distance from the capital: as many as 87 per cent of Cumbrians felt London received too much.[17] But even some Londoners agree: in late 2019, King's College London and the Université de Paris found nearly a third of Londoners thought that their city received more than its fair share and as many as 29 per cent felt that the capital had too much influence on central government decisions.[18]

Spending myths and reality

London does receive a large amount of public investment, but it is an objective fact that the capital contributes far more in taxation than it receives. Both figures are
high. Questions around what constitutes a 'fair share',
however, are much more subjective. In one sense, the
idea that London contributes a great deal to the national
economy but not locally is a misunderstanding of economic reality: London's taxes pay for local investment
across the country. Without the capital's impressive
international business base, much of the tax that pays
for public services would instead be collected in another
world city. In other words, the UK without London
could not currently fund itself. But grievances over
the failure to transform local economies and provide
real opportunities outside of the capital are entirely
legitimate.

Deborah Mattinson's *Beyond the Red Wall* illustrates
how legitimate grievances and genuine misunderstandings can get mixed up. Investigating views in formerly
Labour-voting 'red wall' seats in the north of England,
Mattinson found that 'London came in for special
mention again and again. The resentment cut deep.'
In Accrington, Mattinson was told that, 'the north-
west generates money and it all goes down to London.
We create it, we need it, but they get it.' Many in a

Stoke-on-Trent focus group said that they would never head down to London to shop: 'They're not getting my hard-earned cash down there!'[19]

Relatedly, Professor Anand Menon of the UK in a Changing Europe initiative tells the story of an enlightening interjection at an event on the likely impact of Brexit on the UK economy:

> I was in the northeast, discussing the economics of Brexit. The kind of drop in the United Kingdom's GDP predicted by most economists, I said, would dwarf any savings generated from curtailing contributions to the EU budget. 'That's your bloody GDP,' came the shouted response, 'not ours.'[20]

For Menon, this encapsulated the 'frustration', 'distrust', and 'cynicism' of the 'left behind', but these very real and legitimate feelings do not change reality. London does not receive money from the north-west to fund its infrastructure – in fact, the opposite is true. And 'your GDP' is actually 'our GDP': even when generated in London, the benefits are shared across the nation, paying for hospitals, schools, potholes, and bin collections across the country.

As Mattinson also observed, some feel that London must lose so that they can gain. This is understandable, but it is also untrue. Regional growth is not a zero-sum game. Damaging London's economy would hinder, not help, the nation as a whole. Hence the carefully worded phrase 'levelling up' – which, as Mattinson also found, is something that people in 'red wall' seats say they will believe when they see.[21]

The 'fair share' arguments still stand, though. In October 2020, two-fifths of residents in so-called 'left behind' places across the country felt they were getting 'less than their fair share' of resources; just 4 per cent felt they got more.[22] Contrast this with the one-third of Londoners who agreed with the latter statement. 'Fairness' is subjective, but there is indeed a great deal that is unfair about the operation of the UK economy. Even if there are major misunderstandings, aren't people right to feel that it is unfair that there is so much opportunity in one place and less and less elsewhere? So shouldn't we invest more outside the capital to address this? The answers are, of course, yes and yes, but the national purse still requires that we maintain the capital's ability to support us in the meantime.

A different culture?

'London' can be a code not only for national politics or for the predominant economic system but also for a wider set of cultural values. Some feel that London-based cultural institutions and national media create a 'London-centric' national narrative. In 2014, over three-quarters of UK adults outside London felt that national media was 'very' or 'fairly' focused on London.[23] Efforts to move parts of the BBC and Channel Four out of the capital have come about in response to this accusation, but they have not yet dissipated it.

Do London 'values' exist? We have seen how Londoners are, on average, more socially conservative than widely assumed in some respects, but it is true that London's leaders promote a certain worldview, seeking to reflect their electorate's diversity. Mayor of London Sadiq Khan's 2021 re-election campaign promised to stand up for 'London's values' of 'openness, diversity and tolerance'.[24] The mayor's post-Brexit 'London is Open' campaign promotes these values internationally. But the actions of elites can easily become conflated with the idea that Londoners themselves seek to push their views on those living in the rest of the country. In 2014, columnist Dominic Sandbrook provided a textbook example: 'Londoners spend rather too much time speaking for the nation ... Most of us do not live in London and are sick of having to endure the condescending jibes of those who do.'[25] This strain of anti-Londonism is not just limited to criticism of politicians or the national media, then, but spreads to Londoners themselves.

Nor is anti-Londonism really limited to London. London-based national cultural institutions dominate the national conversation by virtue of being national, rather than being London-based. When a national organisation such as the Premier League or the National Trust takes a 'liberal' stance on an issue, as seen recently during the Black Lives Matter movement, it is accused of metropolitan, liberal bias. But it is also possible that these decisions are the result of senior people thinking long and hard and coming to their own conclusions – not simply because they breathe 'London air'. Indeed, breathing such air did not stop supporters of Millwall FC booing their own players when they 'took a knee' in support of racial equality before a game in December 2020.[26]

As for the National Trust, its headquarters are in Swindon, and yet its decision to review the links between its properties and slavery has led Conservative MP John Hayes to accuse it of being run by an 'out of touch, bourgeois elite' which 'bears no relationship to the sentiments of its members'.[27] This may not be an attack on the capital as such, but it certainly rhymes with one. And still London's reputation suffers. Centre for London found pride in the capital to be significantly lower among non-Londoners than Londoners, with 56 per cent of non-Londoners and 80 per cent of

Londoners saying they were 'very' or 'fairly' proud of London. Feeling proud of the capital city seemed to decline with distance from London.[28] Pride also appears to be reducing over time outside of the capital.[29]

These are far from crisis figures, but they are still alarming. A capital city provides the focal point for a united nation in moments of national celebration, pride, and mourning. It does not have to be universally loved, and nor should it dominate – but it should be a source of national pride, not shame. Its values, surely, should be shared with its nation.

Multiculturalism

Questions about London's perceived cultural dominance invariably intertwine with discussions of London's notable ethnic, religious, and cultural diversity. YouGov polling found that those who held negative perceptions of London were also almost twice as likely as pro-Londoners to agree that 'multiculturalism has had a negative impact on the UK'. In fact, over half of those who hold an unfavourable view of London also hold negative views of multiculturalism.[30] Not all of these negative views will be motivated by racism, but those who are prejudiced against people of other cultures, ethnicities, and religions will – and do – take issue with 'London' because it is home to greater numbers of such people. A similar observation can be made about sexuality: London is the UK region with the highest proportion of people self-identifying as gay, lesbian, or bisexual.[31]

A great deal of resentment of London focuses on its perceived liberal attitudes to multiculturalism and diversity. This can place 'London' on one side of an increasingly, frustratingly stupid 'culture war' that appears to be seeping into national discourse but is actually fought at the keyboards of just a tiny fraction of the population, primarily on social media.[32] While 'London' can be dragged in as target or enemy combatant, the language of this 'war' is often imported from the United States via the 'American internet' and misapplied to the British context.[33] There is actually still a greater tendency towards political moderation in the UK, for example – even if social media can make things feel otherwise.[34] Like Londoners, three-quarters of Brits still think that people from different backgrounds get on well with one another in their local community.[35]

Still, those in positions of power in the capital are perceived by some, online and in the media, as imposing liberal values and diversity on the rest of the nation, whether that be through national policymaking or through news media and entertainment. In recent times, this feeling has reached such a fever pitch that the outrage often seems to predate events: see the online outrage over the reported consideration of playing *Land of Hope and Glory* instrumentally at the Last Night of the Proms[36] or the racial abuse of former Arsenal Women footballer Alex Scott, who was *rumoured* to be replacing Sue Barker as host of the BBC's *A Question of Sport.*[37]

These 'culture wars', while a minority interest in themselves, have been harnessed by political leaders (themselves surely 'elites' by definition) for their own benefit. In August 2017, Conservative MP Jacob Rees-Mogg attacked the 'metropolitan elite rejecting the result of the referendum'.[38] In 2018, Nigel Farage claimed that 'Westminster, the intellectuals, the liberal elite just don't get it' – 'it' also being concerns over immigration.[39] Priti Patel's 2019 speech rejecting the 'North London metropolitan liberal elite' also focused on immigration policy.[40] But does such a metropolitan elite really exist? And does it have distinct, different views from the rest of the country?

Metropolitan elites?

The 'elite' point has some truth to it. The trouble with London is that while most Londoners are far from 'elite', most of the nation's elite are Londoners. There is also a north–south dimension: while poverty and deprivation in England is split fairly evenly between north and south, around 70 per cent of the most affluent are found in the south.[41] But London is home to a particular concentration. Alongside housing the royal family and the most powerful financial centre in the country, London is also the 'world billionaire capital', according to the *Sunday Times Rich List 2020*.[42] The city is also home to around 5,000 of the global 'super rich' – those with upwards of £20 million in disposable non-housing assets – and around 350,000 of its 'wealthy', those with upwards of £700,000.[43]

There is also some truth to the 'metropolitan' point. British Future has found that attitudes to immigration are more positive in the UK's big cities (which just so happen to be where the majority of immigrants live) and that such attitudes become progressively more negative as settlement size decreases.[44] Voting patterns in the EU referendum can also be interpreted as reflecting this notion. However, it is important to note that pro-immigration attitudes are prevalent in most cities, not just London. And at the last census, over 66 per cent of the UK's population lived in local authorities defined as predominantly urban, making city dwellers' views the national majority view.[45]

More significantly, this urban–rural gap in attitudes, while consistent, is not that large. Ranking attitudes to immigration on a scale of one to ten, the difference between the average score in big cities and rural areas was less than one point.[46] Centre for Cities' Andrew Carter observed a similar pattern: in both urban and rural areas, the majority of Brits agree that immigration has made a positive contribution to the UK, economically and culturally. Both also agree that immigration 'means the UK is too full' and that 'services are too stretched'. Again, the differences between urban and rural opinions on each of these issues is a matter of just a few percentage points.[47] What's more, Londoners are far from unquestioningly pro-migration: in late 2019, King's College London polling found that just one in five Londoners think that their city needs more immigration than the current level.[48]

There are other ways in which Londoners have more in common with their compatriots elsewhere in the UK than commonly assumed. In 2012, British Future polling found that 80 per cent of Londoners said they associated the Union Flag with pride and patriotism – the same percentage as across England as a whole (and 2 per cent higher than the overall British average). Londoners also expressed similar opinions about the cross of St George compared to the rest of England.[49] Londoners' views are much closer to the rest of the nation than often assumed. So what is the obsession with London as an out-of-touch centre of 'liberal, metropolitan elite' thought *really* all about?

It may come from a confusion of the views of some of the nation's political and cultural elites with the city in which they work. But it may also be a response to London's notable ethnic and religious diversity. Brits living elsewhere in the country most commonly chose the word 'diverse' to describe Londoners, and it was the third most commonly chosen word to describe London itself.[50] Clearly, the rest of the country notices the capital's diversity. It's possible, then, that there is also some conflation between what the capital *looks like* and what it actually *thinks*. Some of this is surely accidental, but it seems unlikely that those who attack 'metropolitan elites' have not noticed that 'metropolitan' triggers an association with 'non-white' in the minds of Brits.

'Londoners'

For a brief period following the Second World War, the Londoner was viewed as the backbone of the nation. According to historian Jerry White, while 'Londoner' had become a 'slur' in the 1930s, the 'staunch and steadfast' response of the capital's residents in the face of the Blitz 'revalorized "the Londoner" into a title of honour'.[51] Yet recent decades have seen the Londoner recast as an unpatriotic, ignorant 'citizen of nowhere' living within a bubble that speaks only to itself and is unaware of 'real' life in the rest of the country. When BritainThinks set up a 'citizens' jury' in the former 'red wall' in the north of England, tasked with creating its ideal political party, it proposed building a Donald Trump-style wall around the capital: 'They could not have been clearer: keeping Londoners in their place would be a very desirable outcome indeed.'[52]

Some critique of Londoners is light-hearted. The 'Islington dinner party' is often sent up; *Private Eye*'s 'It's Grim Up North London' comic strip has been lampooning out-of-touch Islingtonians since the 1990s. The east London hipster has been the subject of mockery for decades. But in 2018, Centre for London polling found that, after noticing Londoners' diversity, Brits thought Londoners as a whole to be 'arrogant' and 'insular'. Londoners, in contrast, chose 'normal' and 'liberal' to describe themselves and their fellow residents.[53] Still, this divergence can be overstated: the fourth most chosen word by non-Londoners to describe the capital's residents was 'normal', and non-Londoners were not quite as harsh about Londoners as those living in the capital expected them to be.[54] But Londoners are certainly not thought of in exclusively positive terms by those living elsewhere in the UK.

The idea that Londoners 'sneer' at their fellow Brits for their views is also often repeated.[55] The capital's residents are frequently accused of snobbery, including assuming that 'the cleverest people from the north of England all end up in the capital.'[56] As with all stereotypes, there is truth to the notion that some Londoners can be arrogant, but it is unfair and inaccurate to portray the capital's residents in this light. As we know, many Londoners have more in common with their compatriots in the north than they do with the capital's wealthiest residents. And as we saw in Chapter One, there are few places as diverse, as heterogeneous, as London.

Cities vs. 'the rest'

In closing, it is worth noting that while many of the issues between London and its nation state are specific to the UK, some are common across the globe. Other world cities also punch way above their economic weight and generate resentment at home.[57] Greg Clark and Tim Moonen observe that some of these accusations – that such cities get more than their fair share of national resources, that they cause domestic 'brain drain' and exert too much influence on national governments – are often hotly disputed, but 'what is clear is that these concerns pose a major challenge to the viability of the world city model.'[58]

The urbanist Richard Florida connects this situation directly to major political events in the mid-2010s:

The divides separating global superstar cities from the rest of their own countries are exactly what resulted in the voting swings towards Brexit and Trump. Superstar cities, in effect, form a league of their own, often having more in common with each other than they do with cities across their own nations.[59]

Clark and Moonen pick up a similar theme. They observe how political leaders around the world have become increasingly uncertain of how to support their cities amid a reactionary rise in nationalism, separatism, and anti-immigration feeling.[60] Urban–rural divides have been shaping politics in recent years from Italy to Israel, Turkey to Thailand,[61] and these forces have played a part in several geographically divided elections across the globe. In most cases, these divides have very broadly corresponded with 'open', more liberal values in cities and more 'closed', conservative rural areas. In some, the urban masses have lost (2016 EU referendum in the UK; 2016 US presidential election), and in others they have won (2017 French presidential election, 2020 US presidential election).

These divides do not seem likely to disappear any time soon, but two important points should be considered. Firstly, many of these elections turned on extremely tight margins; they were not decisive rejections of these values by all citizens, for all eternity. Brexit was won by a margin of less than two percentage points, and polling now suggests that Brits believe the nation was wrong to leave the EU.[62] None of this is to say the issue is settled – in fact, it is the exact opposite. The great arm-wrestle between populist isolationism and progressive internationalism in the West is currently wavering back and forth around the middle, swinging between 52 and 48 per cent either way. Neither hand has yet come close to bringing the other to the table, and the arrival of COVID-19 has made the outcome even more uncertain.

The second point is that this battle hinges on a relatively small group changing their votes. Most voters continue to vote (boringly) how we would expect them to. Whether it's the 'rust belt' in the US or the 'red wall' in the UK, a decline in traditional industry and associated jobs has left parts of both nations feeling angry at the status quo, and the electoral maps have made these voters, and their concerns, particularly significant for those in the business of winning power. Their problems are genuine, even if not all politicians' promises to address these problems are so. But a successful democracy, and a healthy nation, balances diverse interests in as fair a way as possible; the great arm-wrestle tends towards equilibrium in the centre. In the UK, perhaps it has been drawn too far towards the big cities and the south. This requires adjustment – but over-adjustment could be just as harmful.

4

Pandemic

At the dawn of 2020, London seemed an unstoppable force, a rocket ship shooting away from the rest of its nation. As the first three chapters of this book have highlighted, things were far from perfect – the capital's relationship with the rest of the country was increasingly dysfunctional, and many of its own citizens were struggling – but the overall trajectory of London's population and economic growth was moving consistently upwards, and at a great speed.

Much of the capital's success was powered by its city centre. Each day, the population of Central London would swell by up to 80 per cent as commuters, tourists, shoppers, and day trippers poured in. Together with London's more permanent residents, this group drove the engine of the UK economy. The city centre, covering just 0.01 per cent of the UK's landmass, was responsible for 7 per cent of the nation's jobs and 10 per cent of UK GVA.[1]

There were some signs that not all was well. A drop-off in Tube use suggested that more people were working from home or staying home for entertainment. Alongside the delayed delivery of Crossrail, this decrease had put Transport for London in a financially difficult spot back in 2018.[2] An ongoing shortage of affordable housing was fuelling a growing cost-of-living crisis, making life in the capital less appealing for the highly skilled and mobile, and increasingly impossible for the less well off. There were also substantial tensions between London-wide and national government, with the latter still holding the purse strings. What's more, the UK's expected departure from the EU had damaged London's reputation as a welcoming global city that was open to visitors, students, and international investment – although the capital seemed, thus far, to be weathering the storm surprisingly well.

In other words, London was a premier 'world city' facing a particular manifestation of common 'world city' problems. Yes, there was a notable populist backlash in nations across the world against the things that made a city like London successful. But this was pushback against what seemed to be the inevitable rise of cities as the engines of growth and prosperity. The world was rapidly urbanising, and this trend showed no sign of stopping.[3] London, in decline as recently as the 1980s, was predicted to continue its now decades-long trend of demographic and economic growth.[4]

Then came the coronavirus pandemic.

COVID city

London was put into its first lockdown on 24 March 2020 following a statement by the prime minister the previous evening. The city centre fell eerily silent. Signs went up in pub windows, outside cinemas, and above music venues, all promising to 'be back soon'. But this was a statement of optimism and hope rather than certainty. Workers stayed home, non-essential shops and hospitality were closed, and the once-bustling core of the capital hollowed out almost overnight.

During lockdown, I cycled through Central London. The absence of traffic, both vehicular and human, gave me the opportunity to appreciate the beauty of the city centre and made for wonderful photographs. But the place felt cold and sterile. Despite myself, I missed the bustle, the crowds, and the noise. Piccadilly Circus without people was disorientating and surreal, the South Bank grey and lifeless. The sun shone, the photographs were gorgeous, but the streets and buildings felt dark and ominous.

The capital's public transport system quickly emptied too. London saw a bigger reduction in commuting to workplaces than its global competitors.[5] It is unclear whether this was a sign of strength or weakness: were Londoners more afraid of their city's public transport network, or just more able to adapt to remote working? Either way, London's transport was thrown into crisis. Transport for London's finances, heavily reliant on the fare box, were so badly hit that it required a series of central government bailouts, which came with substantial strings attached. Two government appointees were forced onto Transport for London's board as observers, reasserting central government's involvement in the city's transport.[6]

While spending in Central London's shops and restaurants collapsed, some of the capital's 'local' town centres actually saw an increase in consumer spending during the first lockdown.[7] Still, approximately 30 per cent of Londoners were furloughed at some point during the first wave of the pandemic, a similar figure to the rest of the UK, and those workers were disproportionately located in the boroughs with higher proportions of low-income residents. London's unemployment rate, meanwhile, leapt up more sharply than the UK average between January and June 2020.[8]

London's economic success story has, to date, been driven by the incredible concentration of different functions within its boundaries and the agglomeration benefits of sector-specific clustering. And it's not just London's famous financial services: clusters of creative start-ups in ex-warehouse buildings can be found just moments away from global banks and established multinationals. After daylight hours, the city's culture and nightlife fuel its economy and add to the city's magnetism. Highly skilled, highly mobile people come to London for the employment opportunities but stay for the lifestyle offer, or vice versa.

But this 'ecosystem' proved fragile and complex. As office space fell quiet in the city centre, the coffee shops, pubs, bars, and restaurants followed. So too the museums and galleries, the barbershops and nightclubs. Not all of what ceased would be mourned. Cramped, sweaty rush hour trains were hard to feel nostalgia for. As politicians encouraged workers back to the office to support grab-and-go eateries, others wondered if the 'Pret economy' – whereby well-paid service-sector workers paid over the odds for sandwiches served by their low-paid, often overseas-born equivalents – was such a good thing in the first place.[9]

London now faced existential questions about its future. Would remote working finally lead to the 'death of distance' predicted decades ago when technology first enabled working from home? In turn, would the agglomeration benefits provided by cities cease to matter? Would those residents, suddenly free of regular commuting obligations, flee the city for more affordable, more spacious accommodation in the suburbs and beyond? In driving this process, could coronavirus even aid 'levelling up'?

Some commentators have declared the 'death of the city'.[10] Others predict that the desire for physical proximity will endure beyond the pandemic, despite the substantial medium-term blow dealt to cities and their economies.[11] Either way, firms are reconsidering how much prime city-centre office space they really require.[12] Yet despite much media commentary to the contrary, Centre for London polling in October 2020 found that the vast majority of Londoners intended to stay put in the subsequent twelve months.[13] It will be some time until we know exactly how the pandemic will affect London's future.

'Levelling up' and the pandemic

The effects that the pandemic and its legacy are likely to have on the 'levelling up' agenda, and the capital's relationship with the rest of the UK more broadly, are also uncertain, albeit less so. Talk of COVID-19 as a 'great equaliser', a phrase sometimes used when someone rich or famous contracts the disease, is nonsense. The impact of the pandemic has not been shared equally across society, nor have its effects been geographically equal. The legacy of COVID-19 is likely to be equally unequal.

Despite being hit first and hardest in the 'first wave' of the virus, London also seemed to be the first to recover. After enduring a spike in cases in March/April 2020, by May the number of COVID-19 cases per 100,000 people in London was below that of other UK metropolitan areas, and the subsequent rise in case numbers occurred at a slower rate over the following months than elsewhere.[14] Some suggested that the age profile of London's population, the possible existence of some degree of 'herd immunity' from the first wave, and, perhaps more significantly, the greater proportion of jobs that can be performed from home in the capital explained its resilience. In the final months of 2020, however, a new strain of the virus emerged in London and the southeast, and the capital's fate changed once again.

It is likely that there will be more twists and turns to follow. But while the idea that the capital had acquired immunity seems to have proven fanciful, the sectoral make-up of London's economy and the prevalence of 'knowledge economy' jobs remain an asset. It is for this reason, among others, that the post-pandemic era is likely to see regional inequalities increase rather than reduce. In November 2020, Centre for London found that the capital's economy had been hit harder, and its recovery had been slower, than the rest of the UK.[15] But there is good reason to think that once people are able to travel to work once more and tourism returns, London's economy, with its sizeable talent pool, infrastructure, and built environment, will be in a better position to 'switch back on' than other parts of the country.[16]

The capital's economy will take a major medium-term hit at the very least. The Greater London Authority predicted a drop in London's GVA of 16.8 per cent in 2020.[17] Given HM Treasury's dependence upon London's tax intake for much of its spending across the country, this will be alarming for both capital and country, and will require support for London's economy. The pandemic has also forced the UK government to borrow huge amounts to keep the national economy on life support, which has led to some debate within the government as to whether the country can afford to proceed with the spending spree, designed to assist areas outside of the capital, that the Conservative government pledged in its 2019 manifesto.[18] Regardless, both the pandemic and Brexit have led to an unavoidable but substantial diversion of time and focus away from the 'levelling up' agenda.

So 'levelling up' looks to be under threat – if you believed in it in the first place, that is. Polling from October 2020 found that only 6 per cent of the British public believed that the UK government was 'very committed' to reducing regional inequalities across the country; 28 per cent believed they weren't committed at all.[19] Greater Manchester Mayor Andy Burnham appears to agree with the latter: he has accused the government of reverting to its 'default, London-centric mode' during the crisis, warned that 'levelling up' risked being little more than 'a slogan' without further devolution, and repeatedly used the phrase 'levelling down' to describe central government decisions.[20]

The coronavirus outbreak has both highlighted regional inequalities and exacerbated tensions within the UK. From the differing paths chosen by devolved administrations in Scotland, Wales, and Northern Ireland to the vocal opposition to the UK central government's approach to 'local lockdowns' within England, differences rather than similarities have come to the fore. Burnham was widely and deservedly praised for standing up to central government and making the case for Greater Manchester and the wider north, but his demands were not met.[21] In October 2020, Sadiq Khan claimed that 'the Government's approach of starving the capital of investment will do nothing more than hamper the UK's economic recovery from COVID as a whole.'[22] Tensions are escalating between local and national leaders across the UK, then, including in London.

Some commentators have lamented the return of the polarising rhetoric of the 'north–south divide'.[23] It is indeed a great shame that COVID-19 has highlighted and even increased some divisions alongside rare moments of unity and shared national experience, but this sadly speaks to the great unfairness of the virus itself and its uneven impact. London, given its great importance to the national economy, will need support in order to recover. Equally, if 'levelling up' were to fall off the agenda as a consequence, the country would also suffer.

5

Possibilities

While this book was being written, hopes of a successful COVID-19 vaccine rapidly became reality. The end of this particular pandemic is far from guaranteed, but it could now be in sight. Whether or not coronavirus continues to dominate our lives for some time to come, the 'London problem' faces several potential futures.

It is entirely possible that the impact of the pandemic will see London become even more dominant within the UK, with its dynamic economy able to draw on the capital's talented labour pool and demand for low-skilled labour 'switching back on' with comparative ease once the capital's ecosystem is rebooted. Jobs lost across the rest of the country, meanwhile, may be more likely to vanish permanently. In this case, London will become ever more crucial in sustaining the UK economy, but resentment of the capital is likely to grow.

However, it is also possible that enduring pandemic conditions, or the legacy of these conditions, could lead to a version of the 'death of the city' thesis: an exodus from city centres, including London's; a collapse in the 'ecosystem' that supports culture, hospitality, and other entertainment; increased anti-immigration and anti-globalisation sentiments; and a decline in the willingness of governments to invest in the capital.

This last eventuality would still likely see people and jobs move to London's suburbs and surroundings in the south-east rather than other parts of the country. Like some post-war regional policy that discouraged new development in the capital, this process is more likely to help Reading than Redcar, Harlow rather than Hull, Bromley not Blackpool.[1] It is not impossible that, in time, a depopulating Inner London, starved of investment and no longer the desirable part of the capital, could return to its 1980s-era status as a place of poverty and, potentially, unrest.

Much of this depends on government. The as-yet-unseen impact of the Brexit process will be especially important, in terms of both the economy and the message that it sends to highly skilled migrants. Regardless of the 'Global Britain' rhetoric about welcoming the 'best and brightest', if the UK seems unwelcoming or even hostile towards migrants, then its ability to attract them will be hampered. If skilled people are unwilling to come, it seems likely that tourists, students, and investors will soon follow suit.

Equally, if central government is unwilling to continue to provide the investment that London's recovery requires (particularly in its public transport system), whether for political or practical reasons, the capital's recovery is likely to be slower or incomplete. This would have serious ramifications for the UK economy and, in turn, for central government's ability to deliver its 'levelling up' agenda as currently envisaged. A weaker London, in a 'levelling down' scenario, would see greater regional equality for a period as the capital's economic decline brought it closer in line with the rest of the country, but this would be unlikely to fix the problem in the longer term. All the while, the UK as a whole would become a poorer place, with a smaller tax base raising less money to invest in healthcare, policing, housing, and education.

Moving out?

Token gestures designed to placate anxieties over regional inequalities are often suggested but seem unlikely to address the issue. Centre for Cities has questioned the economic benefit of moving public sector organisations out of the capital.[2] Centre for London polling also showed surprisingly little belief on the part of the British people that doing so would make for a fairer nation.[3] Yet moving the House of Lords or groups of civil servants to other parts of the UK is an easy way to appear to be taking regional inequalities seriously without changing anything too significantly. It is also an easy way to make government less efficient.

As Nick Macpherson, former permanent secretary to the Treasury, has observed, moving civil servants to a struggling town, city, or region is unlikely to make the difference: 'The fact is that it is the private sector which ultimately creates income and wealth, and those regions which do best are the ones which attract skills and capital and create conditions for innovation and enterprise.'[4] For Macpherson, universities can play an important role in fostering successful local economies, but putting public sector jobs into a place can hamper growth, absorbing too much of the local skill base; 'if the public sector was the key to regional prosperity, Northern Ireland would be the richest region in the UK.'[5]

Even moving central government in its entirety would only move the same problem elsewhere – that of a highly centralised bureaucracy attempting to set policy for an entire nation of diverse towns, villages, cities, and rural areas. This is not to say that the idea has no merit whatsoever, rather that moving government and all the various organisations that go with it would be an expensive, time- and energy-consuming process unlikely to have a pay-off that exceeds the cost of disruption. Besides, the idea of moving the UK capital is supported by just one in eight Brits.[6] There is a stronger argument for moving national media and cultural institutions of a national nature, though the agglomeration benefits provided by big cities are simply unavoidable: put simply, the most highly skilled people want to live in places where there is lots to do.

What cities, towns, and villages outside of London and the south-east need is not necessarily the Department of Administrative Affairs to move in, but something a little more entrepreneurial. Improved skills provision is vital; improved connectivity seems important too. Urbanist Edward Glaeser has argued that declining cities like Detroit should simply be left to decline: 'Helping poor people is an appropriate task for government, but helping poor places and poorly run businesses is not.'[7] And yet increasing regional disparities are not just unfair; they can lead to anti-urban and reactionary policies on the part of national governments, with tangible drawbacks for economic growth. It is in everybody's interests, then, for these inequalities to be tackled.

Strong, visionary local leadership certainly seems essential. This is surely best delivered by properly resourced, powerful local government. 'Left behind' communities feel not only that they are missing out on investment in physical and social infrastructure but that decisions over such investment should be taken by local people, not central government.[8] The more power is devolved, the closer decisions are to the people. More powerful city regions could also reduce the dominance of London by creating a national network of regional capitals rather than one dominating in the south-east. Devolution is not by any means a new idea. In 1970, the Conservative Party won a general election on a manifesto that acknowledged that 'people in the regions grow increasingly impatient about the decisions being made in London which they know could be better made locally'; they also pledged to 'devolve government power' to remedy this.[9] Recent manifestos have seen a return to the theme but, with little substantial progress made in the intervening half-century, it seems wise to take current commitments with a pinch of salt.

Whatever approach is taken, Chapter Two of this book has demonstrated that it will take something new and truly special to transform the UK's deeply entrenched regional inequalities. Chapter Three outlined the complex tangle of the threads of anti-Londonism, further demonstrating how hard it is to please everybody and how politically tempting token gestures and harmful anti-London populism may be. But none of this is to say that it isn't worth trying to rebalance the UK away from its capital. As Chapter One describes, there are millions of low-income Londoners who would benefit too.

London's future

What of the capital itself? It seems highly unlikely that London is on the way out. London's long history is full of fire and disease. The capital's density, its great strength in many ways, has also made it vulnerable to repeated crises over centuries. Between the thirteenth and the seventeenth centuries, London had several 'great' fires and 'great' plagues, killing sizeable proportions of its population with alarming regularity, even before the famous events of the 1660s. The nineteenth century saw repeated outbreaks of cholera alongside smallpox and influenza. The twentieth century saw the capital targeted from the air, with over 40,000 Londoners killed by bombs. Even the air itself was a threat: the Great Smog of 1952 directly killed or caused the premature death of thousands more.

While the experience of the Blitz left Londoners temporarily and unusually much-loved by the nation, previous crises did not. When the rich fled London in 1603 due to a particularly bad outbreak of the plague, they were far from well received: 'The sight of a Londoner's flat-cap was dreadful to a lot, a treble ruff threw a village into sweat.'[10] Even the warm national afterglow of the Blitz was extremely short-lived. Peter Hennessy observed that, when the first New Towns were developed in the years immediately following the Second World War, 'the residents of the pleasant, quiet home counties towns affected were less than ecstatic about the proposal of a predominantly working-class cockney influx.'[11]

Yet despite the historic unpopularity of Londoners in their nation, more and more people chose to become Londoners themselves. London's magnetic pull has been so powerful as to eclipse, or at least outweigh, the risks and dangers that came with city life. The dynamism, innovation, and excitement of London life somehow seemingly offset the historically very real chance of death by fire or disease for aspiring Londoners from across the country. Perhaps those who came put this possibility to the back of their mind, hoping that they would be lucky. Maybe they thought that the most recent 'great' fire or 'great' plague was the last. But whether through self-delusion, compulsion and necessity, or a careful balancing of risk and reward, still they came. London predates the United Kingdom and is indeed older than England itself. The city endures, and if we take history as our teacher, London is likely to weather this most recent pandemic too.

So, what does the rest of the country get wrong about London?

The answer to this question is manifold. First, there is little understanding of the extent to which the rest of the UK is dependent upon taxes raised in the capital to fund its local services. The idea that London's growth comes at the expense of the rest of the country is also inaccurate; despite widely held beliefs, there is no finite lump of national 'growth' to be apportioned across the UK. Multiple regions can grow in parallel. The perception that London's dominance is the result of deliberate long-term government intervention is equally flawed – in fact, Chapter Two of this book demonstrated that governments have been attempting to achieve the exact opposite for decades, if not centuries.

Londoners are also much misunderstood. The capital's residents may look and sound different to their counterparts elsewhere in the nation, but they are much more similar in outlook than stereotypes suggest. For example, differences in attitudes towards immigration exist but are relatively small, particularly considering the higher prevalence of immigrants in the city. Despite an increasing national tendency towards polarisation, division, and disagreement, then, Brits inside and outside the capital share more similarities than differences. Equally, the politicians and commentators who attack 'liberal, metropolitan elites' tend to have more in common with those they criticise than they do with the disadvantaged masses that they claim to represent. And, indeed, most Londoners are not rich: many of the nation's elite are Londoners, but a huge number of Londoners are really struggling. Life in the capital is hard for most.

Why we need to learn to stop worrying and to love London (again)

London is the engine of the UK economy, but it is also a centre of culture and innovation. Few cities rival its dynamism. It has grown not because of deliberate, pro-London government policy but because of its appeal to business and individuals alike. This is not to say that central government has never been London-centric in its outlook or decisions in the past – it patently has, generally (but not always) to the benefit of the capital's economic development. London thrives because it is one of a handful of world cities that can compete on the global stage, combining a rich but complex history with hypermodern innovation. London has many recent or short-term assets, but it also has enduring ones, like the English language, the rule of law, Greenwich Mean Time and (until relatively recently, perhaps), an electoral system and political culture that produces strong and stable governance.[12]

London is an elite-level world city, but it is also very much of its nation. So much of the country's history can be found when wandering the capital's streets. London's landmarks are national landmarks, from the Palace of Westminster to St Paul's Cathedral, Shakespeare's Globe to Wembley Stadium. London is an elite world city, but it remains identifiably and uniquely English and utterly British. It is a centre of national culture, show-casing the best the UK has to offer in the arts, science, sport, and ideas. It is not unique in doing so; it is one of several great British cities, but it is the capital. National moments of celebration and solemnity focus on the capital. They could be held anywhere in the UK and be just as special, but they have to be held somewhere, and why not London? London is as English as warm beer, cricket, and cold custard. And the capital's land is surprisingly green and pleasant: somewhere between one-third and almost half of London is green space, depending on which definition you follow. Its connectivity with the rest of the world may mean that the latest global trends and changes hit London first, and the pace of change can be disconcerting, but spend five minutes looking and you will find a deeply English, deeply British city.

Londoners are diverse and heterogenous, but the people of the capital are not as different to the rest of the country as often portrayed. In fact, many of them *are* the rest of the country. They come to the capital to work in highly skilled jobs, to 'level up' themselves and their skills before moving out of London to start families. But Londoners are also elderly, poor, unemployed, and low-paid, working under zero-hours contracts and in the gig economy. London is a huge place, made up of many distinct places, each with individual people in it.

One of the things that makes the capital so special is its mixing of communities, where poverty and wealth sit side by side. Its extremes of inequality can be jarring, and more needs to be done for its most deprived communities, but the opposite – a city segregated into rich and poor districts, or a city of the rich alone – would be appalling. When we talk about diversity and London, we are not just talking about race, ethnicity, or religion, but rather acknowledging that it is still true that, as Dr Johnson so famously said, 'there is in London all that life can afford.'

There are those that are uncomfortable with diversity, and those that seek comfort in the familiar. The pace of change in the capital, whether observed in its rapidly evolving built environment or the faces of new Londoners, can be frightening. Community cohesion is not always easy, and there are of course cracks. The integration and intermingling of London's various communities is an imperfect work in progress. But this work is worth it. Diversity of thought, of experience, of purpose is what drives innovation. Half a million Londoners are of mixed heritage. People of all backgrounds, personalities, perspectives, and experiences come to London to reach their potential without judgement or persecution. Just as many thrive in the relative anonymity that the capital can afford its residents, should they wish to find it, as lament its apparent lack of community (although this too can be found, if only one looks for it).

Many whose talents would otherwise be overlooked succeed in London, such is the lure and the great promise of the city – that and 'the romantic opportunities of population density', as Janan Ganesh delicately puts it, while making a convincing argument that the current 'urban age' is better explained using the language and ideas of Freud than of Marx.[13] People come to the city to meet one another, not just to work together but to get together. There is nowhere better to be single than a big city, and nowhere better to find a partner. For what is the city but the people, and what is the world without love?

There is money and there are careers to be made in arguing that this is all a liberal delusion. But London's success is, and has always been, built on its openness to the world. The diversity of its communities – in every sense of the word – is what makes it what it is. There is national pushback against the very idea of inclusion and openness. This is in large part the result of anti-immigration sentiments being increasingly and inaccurately interwoven with dislike of London's perceived political or economic dominance and the idea of a London-based 'liberal' or 'metropolitan' elite that seeks to impose its views on the rest of the nation. Some of this entangling of different grievances is accidental, but some is deliberate. Either way, this element of anti-London sentiment must be loudly and firmly combatted.

London's economy is an incredible asset, funding schools and hospitals across the country. But it is equally flawed. Its dominance of the UK is undesirable for both capital and country. It is too reliant, still, on financial services as well as on low-paid and insecure work. London is occupied by billionaires and large multinational companies that are regularly accused of not paying their fair share of taxes. But London's contribution to the national purse keeps these islands afloat. There is a very real concern among London's leaders that the political incentive to 'level up' the UK – an important aim, and one no sensible person could disagree with – could lead to central government taking the capital's success for granted.[14] This would be a mistake. Equally, it would be a mistake to abandon the idea of 'levelling up' and allow London to continue to diverge from the rest of the UK unabated. It is in the interests of both capital and country that the UK becomes a more multinodal nation.

In the meantime, recent tides may seem to have turned against London and everything it represents (or is thought to represent). This is concerning. But zooming out to acquire a broader historical perspective, contemporary tidal waves seem barely perceptible ripples, insignificant and short-lived. The long flow of progress has been towards innovation, openness, inclusion, and prosperity. This is not to encourage complacency, by any means, but rather to provide a reminder that calmer waters shall surely return.

It was not long ago that cities were seen as the engines of progress. They are the opposite of isolation. They force us to share. They bring us together.

Anyone can become a Londoner. Anyone can choose not to be one as well. But there is no need to hate the place, and even less justification for hating the people.

London sometimes needs to be a little humbler. This is particularly true of its elites. But it is also time to stand up for itself. It absolutely does not hold a monopoly on any of the things that make it great. But it is great. And it is great for its nation, as well as its citizens.

It is time that we learned to stop worrying and to love London once more.

Acknowledgements

Whilst any issues with this book's contents are my responsibility alone, its research and writing have benefited from the assistance of many. In particular, I would like to extend my thanks to my former colleagues at Centre for London for their support and assistance throughout my time there, and to the students on my MA module on London's history for their constant inspiration. My colleagues at the Strand Group are a constant source of encouragement. I am also extremely grateful to Nick Bowes and Dave Hill for reading a draft of this book, and for their comments and feedback.

This book is dedicated to Grandma, who loved to write. She would have strongly disagreed with its conclusions, but she would have been delighted that I have written it.

Notes

Preface

1. 'When a man is tired of London, he is tired of life', *The Samuel Johnson Sound Bite Page.*
2. 'Dominic Cummings: Stop talking to "rich Remainers"', *BBC*, 10/9/19.
3. 'London draining life out of rest of country – Vince Cable', *BBC*, 19/12/13; and David Maddox, 'Alex Salmond: London is "dark star of the economy"', *The Scotsman,* 4/3/14.

1. People and Place

1. S. Barrett & E. Belcher, 'The London Intelligence Issue 9', *Centre for London*, 25/7/19.
2. 'London's Poverty Profile: 2020', *Trust for London*, 4/20.
3. *Ibid.*
4. S. Katwala, 'Where are the "78% British" headlines about London?' *British Future*, 22/3/13.
5. 'London's Poverty Profile: 2020', *op. cit.*
6. 'Religion in England and Wales 2011', *ONS.*

7. 'Language in England and Wales: 2011', *ONS*.

8. A. Serrant, 'Languages of London, past & present', *Museum of London*, 26/10/18.

9. E. Kaufmann, 'London is less integrated than the rest of the country, a report finds', *LSE Blog*, 2/7/14.

10. 'London and Paris', The Policy Institute, Université de Paris, King's College London & Ipsos MORI, 12/19.

11. S. Katwala, W. Somerville & S. Ballinger, 'Making citizenship matter: Why London needs an Office for Citizenship and Integration', *British Future*, 2/16.

12. 'London and Paris', *op. cit.*

13. N. Bosetti & T. Colthorpe, 'London identities', *Centre for London*, 4/18.

14. H. Sherwood, 'London more religious than rest of Britain, report finds', *The Guardian*, 24/6/20.

15. D. Hill, 'In some ways, London is not as socially liberal as we might think', *OnLondon*, 9/6/19.

16. B. Rogers, 'London's distinctiveness has big implications for national politics', *OnLondon*, 15/11/19.

17. 'EU referendum: The result in maps and charts', *BBC*, 24/6/16.

18. J. Kelly, M. Seymour, T. Moonen, J. Nunley & C. Morrissey, 'Demand and Disruption in Global Cities', JLL and The Business of Cities, 2019.

19. 'Quality of living city ranking', *Mercer*, 2019.

20. R. Strack, M. Booker, O. Kovács-Ondrejkovic, P. Antebi & D. Welch, 'Decoding Global Talent 2018', *BCG*, 25/6/18.

21. M. Ellwood, 'How London Became One of the Best Food Cities in the World', *CN Traveler*, 25/4/16.

22. R. Whitehead with R. Brown, C. Harding, J. Brown, S. Gariban & T. Moonen, 'London at a crossroads', *Centre for London*, 9/20.

23. J. Brown, 'London, UK: Strengthening ties between capital and country', *Centre for London*, 2/19

24. L. McGough & G. Piazza, '10 years of tax', *Centre for Cities*, 7/7/16.

25. C. Giles, 'Why London deserves a thank you note from the rest of Britain', *Financial Times*, 8/6/17.

26. 'Country and regional public sector finances: financial year ending 2019', *ONS*.

27. *Ibid.*

28. *Ibid.*

29. London's GVA per capita is 1.75 times that of the UK average. G. Clark & T. Moonen, *World Cities*

and Nation States (Moscow Urban Forum, 2015), pp.50–97.

30. H. Bessis, 'Competing with the continent: How UK cities compare with their European counterparts', *Centre for Cities*, 9/16.

31. N. Bosetti & J. Brown, 'Head Office: London's rise and future as a corporate centre', *Centre for London*, 5/19.

32. 'Understanding London+ FDI', *London & Partners*, 8/17.

33. 'Traffic statistics', *Heathrow*.

34. '2019 snapshot', *VisitBritain*.

35. 'Understanding the London+ visitor', *London & Partners*, 2016.

36. 'London welcomes record international students in decade as UK becomes most popular overseas study destination', *London & Partners*, 29/1/20.

37. For Boris Johnson, see foreword to 'Growing Together II: London and the UK economy', *Greater London Authority*, 9/14; for Sadiq Khan, see 'There can be no national recovery without a London recovery', *Mayor of London*, 1/10/20.

38. J. Pickford, 'City's former planning chief on why London is "unplannable"', 14/11/14, *Financial Times*.

39. M. Hebbert, *London: More by Fortune than Design* (Chichester: John Wiley & Sons, 1998).

40. T. Travers, *The Politics of London: Governing an Ungovernable City* (London: Palgrave Macmillan, 2003).

41. 'Capital punishments', *Economist*, 18/12/97

42. O. Smith, 'Countries that moved their capitals – and the curious reasons why', *Telegraph*, 27/8/19.

43. A. Davenport & B. Zaranko, 'Levelling up: where and how?' *Institute for Fiscal Studies*, 10/20.

44. See, for example: A. Bounds, 'UK's regional inequality one of worst in developed world', *Financial Times*, 27/11/19.

45. R. Prothero, 'Mind the gap: why the UK might not be the most regionally unequal country', *ONS*, 23/11/18.

46. *Ibid.*

47. 'Analysing regional economic and well-being trends', *ONS*, 25/2/20.

48. S. Clarke, 'London Stalling: Half a century of living standards in London', *Resolution Foundation*, 6/18.

49. G. Bangham & M. Gustafsson, 'The Time of Your Life: Time use in London and the UK over the past 40 years', *Trust for London*, 7/20.

50. J. Brown, 'Transport investment should not be an "either/or" debate', *Centre for London*, 19/8/19.
51. 'Annual personal well-being estimates', *ONS*, 30/7/20.
52. Davenport & Zaranko, *op. cit.*
53. 'Analysing regional economic and well-being trends', *op. cit.*
54. M. Ward, 'Rebalancing the economy: prospects for the North', *The Smith Institute*, 3/11.
55. 'London's Poverty Profile', *op. cit.*
56. D-R. Srblin, 'Child Poverty in London', *Child Poverty Action Group*, 22/2/18.
57. 'London's Poverty Profile', *op. cit.*
58. *Ibid.*
59. D. Smith, 'Mapping Patient Data to Consider the Role of Geography in Public Health', *Imperial College London*, 2012.
60. S. Clarke, 'London Stalling', *op. cit.*
61. *Ibid.*
62. 'State of the Nation 2017: Social Mobility in Great Britain', *Social Mobility Commission*, 11/17.
63. 'Qualifications of working age population', *London Datastore*, 12/19.
64. K. Hecht, D. McArthur, M. Savage & S. Friedman, 'Elites in the UK: Pulling Away? Social mobility,

geographic mobility and elite occupations', *The Sutton Trust*, 1/20.

65. *Ibid.*

66. A repeated theme in Jerry White's excellent histories of the capital, but particularly in J. White, *London in the Twentieth Century: A City and its People* (London: Vintage, 2008).

2. Politics and Policy

1. 'Growing Together II: London and the UK economy', *op. cit.*

2. B. Johnson, 'PM Economy Speech', *gov.uk*, 30/6/20.

3. J. Harris & J. Domokos, 'Working-class voters desert Labour as "red wall" crumbles', *The Guardian*, 13/12/19.

4. 'Get Brexit Done; Unleash Britain's Potential: The Conservative and Unionist Party Manifesto 2019', *Conservative Party*, 2019.

5. 'Forward, Together, Our Plan for a Stronger Britain and a Prosperous Future: The Conservative and Unionist Party Manifesto 2017', *Conservative Party*, 2017.

6. 'Strong Leadership, A Clear Economic Plan, A Brighter, More Secure Future for Northern Ireland', *Conservative Party*, 2015.

7. Davenport & Zaranko, *op. cit.*

8. S. E. Rasmussen, *London: The Unique City* (Cambridge, MA: MIT Press, 1988), pp. 67–75.

9. J. Ferris & A. Thrush, 'London', *The History of Parliament*.

10. J. Tucker, *Four Letters on Important National Subjects* (London: R. Raikes, 1783), p.45.

11. *Ibid.*, p.48.

12. J. Brown, 'London, UK', *op. cit.*

13. P. Hall, *Cities in Civilisation* (London: Phoenix, 1999), p.657.

14. J. White, *London in the Nineteenth Century: 'A Human Awful Wonder of God'* [ebook edn] (London: Vintage, 2011).

15. E. Howard, *Garden Cities of Tomorrow* (London: Swan, Sonnenschein & Co., 1902), p.11.

16. White, *London in the Twentieth Century*, *op. cit.*, pp.36–7

17. R. Martin, A. Pike, P. Tyler & B. Gardiner, 'Spatially Rebalancing the UK Economy: Towards a New Policy Model?' *Regional Studies* (2016) 50:2, p.345.

18. *Ibid.*

19. M. Barlow, 'The Dispersal of Industry', *Spectator*, 1/3/40.

20. P. Abercrombie, *Greater London Plan 1944* (London: HMSO, 1945), p.57

21. White, *London in the Twentieth Century, op. cit.*, p.40.

22. J. Mitchell, 'A chaos of areas and bodies: the English dimension' in J. Mitchell, *Devolution in the UK* (Manchester: MUP, 2009), pp.102–3.

23. White, *London in the Twentieth Century, op. cit.*, p.40.

24. *London Government Act 1973*, s.73.

25. White, *London in the Twentieth Century, op. cit.*, p.52.

26. 'Conservative General Election Manifesto 1979', *Conservative Party*, 1979.

27. J. Taylor & C. Wren, 'UK Regional Policy: An Evaluation', *Regional Studies* (1997) 31:9, p.838.

28. R. Martin et al., 'Spatially Rebalancing the UK Economy', *op. cit.*, p.346.

29. R. Vinen, *Thatcher's Britain: The Politics and Social Upheaval of the 1980s* (London: Simon & Schuster, 2009), p.182.

30. A. Carrascal-Incera, P. McCann, R. Ortega-Argilés & A. Rodríguez-Pose, 'UK Interregional Inequality in a Historical and International Comparative Context', *National Institute Economic Review* (2020) 253, pp.R4–R17.

31. R. Martin et al., 'Spatially Rebalancing the UK Economy', *op. cit.*, p.346.

32. 'Gordon Brown's Mansion House Speech', *Guardian*, 22/6/6.

33. R. Martin, 'Rebalancing the Spatial Economy: The Challenge for Regional Theory', *Territory, Politics, Governance* (2015) 3:3, p.237.

34. L. Dalingwater, 'Regional Performance in the UK under New Labour', *Observatoire de la société britannique* (2011) 10, pp.115–136.

35. P. Mandler, 'Britain's EU Problem is a London Problem', *Dissent*, 24/6/16.

36. I. R. Gordon, 'Quantitative easing of an international financial centre: how central London came so well out of the post-2007 crisis', *Cambridge Journal of Regions, Economy and Society* (2016) 9:2, pp.335–353.

37. Although politicians had fallen hard, bankers were making a surprising comeback. See Ipsos MORI, 'Trust in politicians falls sending them spiralling back to the bottom of the Ipsos MORI Veracity Index', *Ipsos MORI*, 26/11/19.

38. 'Invitation to join the government of Britain', *Conservative Party*, 2010.

39. 'Cities Outlook 2019', *Centre for Cities*.

40. R. Martin et al., 'Spatially Rebalancing the UK Economy', *op. cit.*, p.343.
41. R. Martin, 'Rebalancing the Spatial Economy', *op. cit.*, p.238.
42. S. Jeffrey, 'Has the Northern Powerhouse been a success?', *Centre for Cities*, 27/6/19.
43. 'The *Guardian* view on toxic relations between London and the rest of the UK', *Guardian*, 16/9/14.
44. R. Mason, 'Losing UKIP councillor blames poor London polls on "cultured elite"', *Guardian*, 23/5/14.
45. 'Farage "felt awkward" on train', *Evening Standard*, 28/2/14.
46. J. Harris, 'London has become a citadel, sealed off from the rest of Britain', *Guardian*, 14/4/14.
47. For example: H. Mance, 'A singular case for London independence', *Financial Times*, 3/10/17.
48. J. O'Malley, 'Declare London independent from the UK and apply to join the EU', *Change.org* 2016.
49. YouGov/Evening Standard Survey Results, YouGov, 5/7/16.
50. D. Lammy, 'London must look to be a city-state if hard Brexit goes ahead', *Evening Standard*, 20/3/17.
51. 'Forward, Together, Our Plan for a Stronger Britain and a Prosperous Future', *op. cit.*

52. L. Raikes, 'Future Transport Investment in the North', *IPPR North*, 1/18.

53. J. Brown, 'Transport investment should not be an "either/or" debate', *op. cit.*

54. J. Williams, 'Huge fires have consumed northern moors for a week. Why the silence from London's media?', *New Statesman*, 2/7/18; and A. Burnham, 'As the Northern rail crisis worsens, Grayling is asleep at the wheel', *The Times*, 1/6/18.

55. 'Funding', *Crossrail 2*.

56. J. Brown, 'The government's Stronger Towns Fund ignores London's poor communities', *OnLondon*, 6/3/19.

57. 'Sadiq Khan condemns government's "abject failure" on housing', *Mayor of London*, 23/11/17; and P. Crerar, 'Sadiq Khan: Theresa May is most anti-London PM since Margaret Thatcher', *Evening Standard*, 5/5/17.

58. 'Theresa May's Keynote speech at Tory conference in full', *Independent*, 5/10/16.

59. 'Whingeing. Contemptuous. Unpatriotic. Damn the Bremoaners and their plot to subvert the will of the British people', *Mail Online*, 12/10/16.

60. 'Get Brexit Done; Unleash Britain's Potential', *op. cit.*

61. D. Hill, 'Lack of government strategy is real blockage to "levelling up" regions, says new report', *OnLondon*, 28/9/20.

62. J. Brown, T. Travers & R. Brown, *London's Mayor at 20: Governing a global city in the 21st century* (London: Biteback, 2020), pp.325–7.

63. G. Pogrund & T. Shipman, 'Treasury's new branch... in Darlington', *The Times*, 4/10/20.

64. S. Payne & G. Parker, 'The smashing of the British state', *Financial Times*, 8/10/20.

65. M. D'Arcy, 'House of Lords: Will the chamber really move to York?' *BBC*, 16/7/20.

66. Hansard, HL vol 778, col 473 (23/1/17).

67. Hansard, HL vol 788, cols 63–4 (8/1/18).

68. N. Crafts, 'Regional GDP in Britain, 1871–1911: Some Estimates', *Scottish Journal of Political Economy* (February 2005) 52:1, pp.59–61.

69. *Ibid.*, p.63.

70. J. Brown, 'London, UK', *op. cit.*

71. A. Carrascal-Incera et al., *op. cit.*, p.R14.

72. *Ibid.*

73. R. Martin et al., 'Spatially Rebalancing the UK Economy', *op. cit.*, p.346.

74. D. Edgerton, 'The Brexiteers' greatest trick was convincing the old they hated Brussels more than London', *New Statesman*, 7/8/19.

3. Perceptions and Prejudices

1. R. Liddle, 'It's official: we all hate London. Could it be the greed, the elitism or the hypocrisy?', *The Times*, 9/2/20.

2. *Ibid.*

3. D. Goodhart, *The Road to Somewhere: The New Tribes Shaping British Politics* [ebook edn] (London: Penguin, 2017).

4. *Ibid.*

5. P. Collier, 'How to save Britain from London', *Prospect*, 12/10/18.

6. P. Mandler, 'Britain's EU Problem is a London Problem', *op. cit.*; and D. Edgerton, 'The Brexiteers' greatest trick was convincing the old they hated Brussels more than London', *op. cit.*

7. Private interview, August 2018.

8. ITV News, 'Does the North-South divide still exist? [video]', *YouTube* (uploaded 25/2/19).

9. M. Smith, 'Where is London most and least popular?', *YouGov*, 25/6/18.

10. J. Brown, 'London, UK', *op. cit.*

11. For example: T. Hazeldine, 'London punishing the north is no accident: it's how England is run', *Guardian*, 19/10/20.

12. And see, for example: J. Brunsden, 'UK and EU to resume talks in final push for post-Brexit trade

deal', *Financial Times*, 22/10/20; or B. Moens, 'Brussels accuses London of selfish obstinance in Brexit talks', *Politico*, 2/9/20.

13. 'English Devolution Poll', *Survation*, 25/3/14.

14. Z. Wilcox, N. Nohrovà & E. Bidgood, 'City Views: How do Britain's cities see London?', *Centre for Cities & Centre for London*, 5/14.

15. 'Polling on resident satisfaction with councils: Round 20', *Local Government Association*, 6/18.

16. J. Brown, 'London, UK', *op. cit.*

17. M. Smith, 'London gets more than its fair share of public spending, say most Britons', *YouGov*, 8/2/19.

18. M. Kleinman, J. Brown & B. Page, 'How Londoners and Parisians saw their cities on the eve of the pandemic', *King's College London*, 23/10/20.

19. D. Mattinson, *Beyond the Red Wall: Why Labour Lost, How the Conservatives Won and What Will Happen* (London: Biteback, 2020), pp.24–5.

20. A. Menon, '2016: A review', *UK in a Changing Europe*, 31/12/16.

21. Mattinson, *Beyond the Red Wall*, *op. cit.*, pp.147–8.

22. '"Left behind" areas missing out on community facilities and places to meet', *Local Trust*, 10/20.

23. Z. Wilcox et al., *op. cit.*

24. S. Khan, 'Standing up for London', *Sadiq for London 2021*.

25. D. Sandbrook, 'His policies fill me with dread. But this is what you get when a smug metropolitan elite treat the people with contempt', *Mail Online*, 24/5/14.

26. 'Millwall 0–1 Derby: Game overshadowed by fans booing players taking a knee before kick-off', *BBC*, 6/12/20.

27. C. Hope, 'National Trust faces anger after chairman defends Black Lives Matter movement', *Telegraph*, 6/11/20.

28. J. Brown, 'London, UK', *op. cit.*

29. A. Gimson, R. Jolley, S. Katwala, P. Kellner, A. Massie & R. Miranda, 'This Sceptred Isle: Pride not prejudice across the nations of Britain', *British Future*, 5/21.

30. M. Smith, 'Where is London most and least popular?', *op. cit.*

31. D. Hill, 'In some ways, London is not as socially liberal as we might think', *op. cit.*

32. M. Savage, '"Culture wars" are fought by tiny minority – UK study', *Guardian*, 24/10/20.

33. H. Lewis, 'The World is Trapped in America's Culture War', *The Atlantic*, 27/10/20.

34. M. Savage, '"Culture wars" are fought by tiny minority – UK study', *op. cit.*

35. 'Fears of social divisions re-emerging as lockdown unity fades', *British Future*, 18/6/20.

36. A. Finnis, 'Rule, Britannia and Land of Hope and Glory lyrics: How the bizarre "row" over the Last Night of the Proms gained momentum', *i News*, 25/8/20.

37. L. Bakare, 'Alex Scott gets racist abuse over Question of Sport speculation', *Guardian*, 18/9/20.

38. *Ibid.*

39. R. Logan, 'Rees-Mogg FURIOUS at Starmer on Brexit: "Metropolitan elite are REJECTING the referendum"', *Express*, 3/8/17.

40. 'Home Secretary speech to Conservative conference', *Channel 4 News*, 1/10/19.

41. D. Smith, 'Levelling up is hard to do – as the prime minister is about to discover', *The Times,* 30/12/20.

42. R. Watts, 'Rich List 2020: Britain's wealthiest lose billions to coronavirus', *The Times*, 16/5/20.

43. R. Atkinson, 'How the super rich conquered London', *The Conversation*, 28/5/20.

44. J. Rutter & R. Carter, 'National Conversation on Immigration', *British Future*, 9/18, p.32.

45. 'The 2011 Rural-Urban Classification for Local Authority Districts in England', *Government Statistical Service*, 2017.

46. J. Rutter & R. Carter, 'National Conversation on Immigration', *op. cit.*, p.32.
47. A. Carter, 'Does the metropolitan elite really exist?' *The Times*, 22/6/18.
48. 'London and Paris', *op. cit.*
49. 'The myth of "planet London"', *British Future*, 3/5/12.
50. J. Brown, 'London, UK', *op. cit.*
51. White, *London in the Twentieth Century*, *op. cit.*, pp.102–3.
52. Mattinson, *Beyond the Red Wall*, *op. cit.*, p.25.
53. 'YouGov/Centre for London Survey Results', *Centre for London*, 3/9/18–4/9/18; and YouGov/ Queen Mary University London Survey Results, *Centre for London*, 3/9/18–7/9/18.
54. J. Brown, 'London, UK', *op. cit.*
55. S. Moore, 'London as a separate city-state? The capital needs to check its privilege', *Guardian*, 25/6/16.
56. H. Pidd, 'Don't sneer at northerners for voting for Brexit – there are sound reasons', *Guardian*, 9/12/16.
57. G. Clark & T. Moonen, *World Cities and Nation States*, *op. cit.*, p.41.
58. *Ibid.*

59. R. Florida, *The New Urban Crisis: Gentrification, Housing Bubbles, Growing Inequality, and What We Can Do About It* (London: Oneworld, 2017), p.19.

60. G. Clark & T. Moonen, *World Cities and Nation States, op. cit.*, p.15.

61. G. Rachman, 'Urban-rural splits have become the great global divider', *Financial Times*, 30/7/18; and D. Kopf, 'The rural-urban divide is still the big story of American politics', *Quartz*, 6/11/20.

62. YouGov/The Times Survey Results, *YouGov*, 11/11/20–12/11/20.

4. Pandemic

1. J. Brown, S. Gariban, E. Belcher & M. Washington-Ihieme, 'Core Values: The Future of Central London', *Centre for London*, 2/20.

2. T. Powley, 'Transport for London on course for £1bn deficit', *Financial Times*, 26/2/18.

3. '68% of the world population projected to live in urban areas by 2050, says UN', *UN*, 16/5/18.

4. 'The London Plan (Intend to Publish): Spatial Development Strategy for Greater London', *Mayor of London*, 12/19.

5. 'The London Intelligence', *Centre for London*, 8/20.

6. J. Brown, T. Travers & R. Brown, *London's Mayor at 20*, op. cit., pp.325–8.

7. 'The London Intelligence', *Centre for London*, 8/20, *op. cit.*

8. *Ibid.*

9. S. O'Connor, 'Goodbye to the "Pret economy" and good luck to whatever replaces it', *Financial Times*, 1/9/20.

10. A. Hernández-Morales, K. Oroschakoff & J. Barigazzi, 'The death of the city', *Politico*, 27/7/20.

11. E. Glaeser in CentreForLondon, 'End of an era? Edward Glaeser on cities after coronavirus: The London Conference 2020 [video]', *YouTube* (uploaded 2/11/20).

12. 'Barclays boss: Big offices "may be a thing of the past"', *BBC*, 29/4/20.

13. N. Bosetti & E. Belcher, 'The London Intelligence – Snapshot of Londoners – October 2020', *Centre for London*, 21/10/20.

14. 'The London Intelligence', *op. cit.*

15. N. Bosetti, E. Belcher & N. Quarshie, 'The London Intelligence – London Economic Tracker – November 2020', *Centre for London*, 19/11/20.

16. P. Swinney, 'Is Covid ending London's growth miracle?' *Centre for Cities*, 29/10/20.

17. 'London: not falling down', *Financial Times*, 31/8/20.

18. F. Elliott & O. Wright, 'Coronavirus makes Tories pause on levelling up', *The Times*, 24/10/20.

19. 'How committed do you think the UK government are, if at all, to reducing regional inequalities across the country?', *YouGov*, 27/10/20.

20. G. Grylls, 'Levelling up just a slogan, say Andy Burnham and Steve Rotheram', *The Times*, 22/10/20; A. Burnham, 'Are we all in this together? It doesn't look like it from the regions', *Guardian*, 16/5/20; and H. Carter, 'Andy Burnham accuses government of "levelling down" the north and releasing the national lockdown "too early"', *Manchester Evening News*, 25/9/20.

21. For example: Z. Forsey, '"King of the North" Andy Burnham labelled hero for fighting against Tories – "this is what leadership looks like"', *Mirror*, 20/10/20; and A. Haddow, 'In praise of Andy Burnham, the King of the North who told the Tories to fuck off (we're paraphrasing)', *NME*, 22/10/20.

22. 'There can be no national recovery without a London recovery', *Mayor of London*, 1/10/20.

23. R. Crampton, 'The north-south divide is great fun, till it starts turning nasty', *The Times*, 24/10/20.

5. Possibilities

1. I apologise for these slightly tortured lists, but I find them irresistible.
2. P. Swinney & G. Piazza, 'Should we move public sector jobs out of London?' *Centre for Cities*, 10/8/17.
3. J. Brown, 'London, UK', *op. cit.*
4. N. Macpherson, 'The case against further devolution', *King's College London*, 24/7/19.
5. *Ibid.*
6. M. Smith, 'Britons don't want to see London lose capital status', *YouGov*, 27/11/18.
7. E. Glaeser, *Triumph of the City* (Macmillan, 2011), p.249.
8. '"Left behind" areas missing out on community facilities and places to meet', op. cit.
9. '1970 Conservative Party General Election Manifesto: A Better Tomorrow', *Conservative Party*.
10. C. Hibbert & B. Weinreb eds., *The London Encyclopaedia*, op. cit., p.618.
11. P. Hennessy, *Never Again: Britain 1945–51* (London: Penguin, 2006), pp.172–3.

12. As outlined in N. Bosetti & J. Brown, 'Head Office: London's Rise and Future as a Corporate Centre', op. cit.
13. J. Ganesh, 'Sex and the cities', *Financial Times*, 20/11/20.
14. J. Pickard, 'London's leaders warn over push to narrow regional inequalities', *Financial Times*, 12/1/20.

HAUS CURIOSITIES

Inspired by the topical pamphlets of the interwar years, as well as by Einstein's advice to 'never lose a holy curiosity', the series presents short works of opinion and analysis by notable figures. Under the guidance of the series editor, Peter Hennessy, Haus Curiosities have been published since 2014.

Welcoming contributions from a diverse pool of authors, the series aims to reinstate the concise and incisive booklet as a powerful strand of politico-literary life, amplifying the voices of those who have something urgent to say about a topical theme.